The views and opinions expressed in this book are solely those of the Author and do not reflect the views of the Publisher. The Author's opinions are based on their own research, experiences, and perspective. The Publisher does not assume any responsibility or liability for any errors (factual or otherwise), inaccuracies, omissions, or consequences arising from the use of the information contained within this book. Readers are encouraged to independently verify the information and consult with appropriate professionals before making any decisions, forming any opinion or taking any actions based on the contents of this book.

Accounting And Financial Frauds – The What, The How And The Why

(With 50 Case Studies)

Authored by

CA Uday Gandhi
FCA, Member of ACFE
Empanelled Forensic Auditor
Government of Maharashtra
Indian Banking Association (IBA)

Copyright © 2023 by Uday Shantilal Gandhi

All rights reserved.

This book or any portion thereof may not be reproduced or used in any manner whatsoever without the express written permission of the respective writer of the respective content except for the use of brief quotations in a book review.

The writer of the respective work holds sole responsibility for the originality of the content and The Write Order is not responsible in any way whatsoever.

Printed in India

ISBN: 978-93-5996-311-2

First Printing, 2023

The Write Order

A division of Nasadiya Technologies Private Ltd.

Koramangala, Bangalore

Karnataka-560029

THE WRITE ORDER PUBLICATIONS.

www.thewriteorder.com

Edited by Anagha

Typeset by MAP Systems, Bengaluru

Book Cover designed by Sankhasubhro Nath

Publishing Consultant - Deeksha

Chapter 1 of this book offers a journey into the world of accountancy and financial statements, such as the Balance Sheet, Profit & Loss Account, Cash Flow Statements, etc. It has been included especially for those readers without any accounting background.

The book unravels various types of financial fraud that are commonly perpetrated, along with their modus operandi. These insights are largely based on the author's knowledge and extensive experience in forensic audit.

Emphasis is also placed on practical cases of fraud detected in India and abroad. This will provide readers with a ring-side view of the reasons behind and the methods employed in these actual cases.

When explaining case studies, specific items related to the Profit & Loss account and Balance Sheet are highlighted. This sheds light on how fraud was committed through the manipulation of such financial statements. Relevant sections of The Indian Penal Code, 1860 (IPC) are also referred to and explained for the benefit of the reader.

Furthermore, the author has taken into consideration the requirements of investigating officers while narrating this book.

Forewords

Sri Uday Gandhi, a leading Chartered Accountant, based out of Mumbai and an accredited forensic auditor, has rendered a seminal service in publishing a book on Accounting and Financial frauds.

I have worked with Sri Uday Gandhi closely right from the time I was Commissioner of Police, Mumbai, where his knowledge of accounting and auditing skills were stellar, to say the least.

It is lucidly written and in layman's language explains each and every detail about Financial Statements, Balance Sheets and a tool kit for dissecting the most intricate financial frauds. The manner in which 50 case studies pertaining to real bank frauds, share scams etc, have been compiled and explained, is highly illuminating.

I can safely say that I have not come across such a comprehensive, simple and professional book on the subject, so far.

Shri Arup Patnaik, IPS (Rtd.)
Former Commissioner of Police (Mumbai)
Former DG Maharashtra

. . . .

The hallmark of the Book "Accounting and Financial Frauds" is it's simple language which can be understood even by non accounting professionals and it's powerful narrative of various case studies, which were presented in a lucid manner. The Book unravels various types of financial frauds that are commonly perpetrated, along with their modus-operandi. These insights are largely based on Sh. Gandhi's own experiences in cracking several financial frauds.

Shri B V Gopinath, IRS (Rtd.)
Former Pr. Chief Commissioner of Income Tax

. . . .

We increasingly hear and read about accounting and financial scams, not just by individuals but also by listed companies and even by banks. Sadly, most of us, while aghast at the humongous sums involved, are not able to fully comprehend the modus operandi or the weak spots in the financial system that the perpetrators have taken advantage of. This book by Mr. Uday Gandhi is therefore a timely initiative. It covers the wide spectrum of accounting and financial frauds in an easy-to-understand format. The book not only educates, but also illustrates.

Shri Madhu Mohan Damodhar, I.R.S (Rtd.)
Mem CESTAT (Rtd.)

. . . .

This book is an indispensable resource for anyone seeking to understand, combat, and prevent financial fraud. The book will also serve as a reliable guide to anyone looking to identify the early red flags by using simple tools such as ratio analysis.

Readers that do not have a background in accounting and finance will especially appreciate how the author has tried to simplify each element of financial reporting and demystified the complex schemes used to commit fraud with the help of real world case studies.

Best Wishes,
Shri Sushil Agrawal
CFO, Aditya Birla Group

....

Shri Uday Gandhi is a learned Chartered Accountant by profession and is a very reliable forensic auditor. I have had several occasions during my long stint in Economic Offence Wing of Mumbai Police, both as Additional Commissioner of Police and thereafter as Joint Commissioner of Police to work with him and assign him highly sensitive and complex cases like National Stock Exchange Limited (NSEL) scam and many other such cases.

Mr. Gandhi's present book "Accounting and Financial Frauds" which is written in such a simple and interesting way that even a person without any background in commerce, finance or economics can easily understand and refer to while going through balance-sheet. I find this book to be very handy for police officers and other investigating agencies throughout the country and even abroad. I hope that in future Mr. Gandhi will come forward with many such interesting handbooks and compendium, which will go a long way in being part of training manuals even for Police Training Institutes across the country. I wish him all the success in his future endeavour.

Shri Rajvardhan
Additional DG & Joint Managing Director
Maharashtra State Security Corporation
Mumbai

....

Shri Uday Gandhi is decidedly "a chartered accountant by profession but an investigator at heart". This is the only surmise that explains how over the years he has effortlessly blended his auditing training to the demanding and sometimes intuitive needs of criminal investigations and law. His rich experience of an accounting and auditing career has been interwoven with tantalizing forensic experience working on sensational economic offences with leading law enforcement agencies of the country. His bandwagon consists of not only professional expertise but also an uncanny ability to communicate important and complicated facts in a simple, cogent and lucid style. This puts him in an eminently enviable position to bring out this immensely useful book which logically takes the reader from a journey of accounting concepts to their relevance to accounting frauds flavoured subsequently with important case studies.

I have been privileged to have Shri Gandhi in my team as a forensic expert during my stints as Joint CP EOW Mumbai and as Addl. Director General, Anti-Corruption Bureau, Maharashtra State and can state unstintingly that his professional sincerity and enthusiasm percolates to all tasks that he undertook and the same qualities find reflection in the present book. I would also urge him to bring out the same in vernacular to expand the reach and scope of the book and wish him the very best on his inceptive steps as a writer

Shri Niket Kaushik
ACdl. Director General,
Anti-Corruption Bureau,
Maharashtra State.

. . . .

It is indeed a pleasure and a privilege to write the foreword for the path breaking efforts put in by C.A. Shri. Uday Gandhi in compiling his path breaking book "Accounting and Financial Frauds".

While there is no dearth of publications on the subject of Accounting and Forensic auditing, there is an immensely felt need for a hand book which caters to the investigation of financial crimes. It is trite to mention that the overwhelming majority of investigators have insufficient exposure in the subject of accounting and book keeping. This becomes a challenge in arriving at the core issues which need to be investigated in a financial crime. It is this interface of the criminal law and financial illegalities which has been explored in a very crisp manner by Shri Gandhi's book. Even otherwise, his assistance, advice and cooperation to the department have been exemplary. Irrespective of his official engagement Shri Gandhi has always cheerfully agreed to render his professional services for the cause of EOW, Mumbai.

I am sure that this book will serve as a guide, if not "The guide" for the future investigation of financial crime in India.

I wish him all the best in his future endeavours.

Shri. Nishith Mishra, I.P.S.
Joint Commissioner of Police
Economic Offence Wing
Mumbai

. . . .

Shri. Uday Gandhi has concised his forensic audit expertise and knowledge for the benefit of Economic Offence Investigators. His choice of case studies has opened up the ingenuity of those minds that has played with thoughts of innocent & unexpecting people.

The concepts, jargons and case studies are explained lucidly and are easy to understand. This book will equally be appreciated by investigators and general readers.

Shri Jaykumar IPS,
Joint Commissioner of Police,
Mumbai.

. . . .

Dear Uday,

I believe that your book is the need of the hour in today's world, where financial frauds are becoming increasingly common, it is crucial to have a comprehensive resource that provides guidance on how to investigate such cases. Your book fills this gap perfectly.

I also want to commend you on the vast variety of frauds covered in your book. From Ponzi schemes to bank frauds to IPOs, you leave no stone unturned. This extensive coverage ensures that readers get a holistic understanding of the different types of financial frauds.

I want to express my sincere appreciation for your work on "Accounting and Financial Frauds: the what, the how and the why " Your book is a valuable resource for professionals and individuals interested in understanding and combating financial frauds. I have no doubt that it will make a significant contribution to the field.

Shri Shailesh Bathiya
Senior Chartered Accountant
Legal Bathiya

. . . .

Mr. Uday Gandhi's book on "Accounting and Financial Frauds" is an absolutely revealing account of how the banks and financial institutions are taken for a ride.

What is more important is that Mr. Gandhi has explained it in a simple language that can be understood by a layman. In this book he has explained the basics of accountancy and role expected of a bank auditor. Expectations from the auditors by the society as a whole are huge.

Mr. Gandhi as a professional forensic auditor and investigator has discharged his duties diligently. This book provides reader a glimpse into his work. It is a reference manual for next generation.

Shri CV Deodhar,
Senior Chartered Accountant

....

The most important about this book is Mr Gandhi has been able to explain the modus operandi in simple language. The examples that he has chosen are eye openers.

The book also explains the importance of audit, internal controls, checks and balances and other procedures that has to be adopted by the system.

Financial crooks use various ways and means to commit crime. Mr Gandhi has correctly documented them and has thoroughly exposed them.

Shri Sunil Deodhar

....

Shree Uday Gandhi has brought out a book on economic frauds as a time when it's most needed. As we soon evolve into being a developed nation it's important that our regulatory and investigative checks are strengthened.

Uday's experience of decades in assisting forensic investigations have brought out an extremely useful bible for all law makers and enforcers, forensic auditors, bankers and corporate Indians.

I'm certain this book shall be an extremely useful tool to one and all and would urge Uday to update this every few years and continue to enhance our understanding and skill as we navigate our countries rapid progress.

Shri Chandir Gidwani
Founder & Chairman Emeritus
Centrum Capital.

. . . .

Contents

Chapter 1: Financial Statement Of The Company 1

1.1 What Is A Balance Sheet? 2

1.2 What Is a Profit & Loss Account? 14

1.3 What Are Cash Flow Statement And Fund Flow Statements? 24

1.4 Contingent Liabilities 28

1.5 What Are Notes To Accounts? 28

Chapter 2: Auditor's & Director's Roles And Responsibilities .. 29

2.1 Appointment Of Auditors (Section 139
     Of Companies Act, 2013) 29

2.2 Auditors' Report under CARO 31

2.3 Qualified Audit Report 38

2.4 Criminal Liability Of Auditors 39

2.5 Sections Of Companies Act, 2013 Related To Directors 40

2.6 Role Of Directors 41

2.7 Criminal Liability Of Directors 42

2.8 Appointment Of Foreign National As Director
   In Indian Company 45

2.9 Fiduciary Duty Of Directors 47

2.10 Independent Directors – Appointment, Roles,
   And Criminal Liabilities 48

Chapter 3: Forensic Accounting & Auditing 51

3.1 What Is Forensic? 51

3.2 What Is Forensic Auditing? 51

3.3 What Is Fraud? 52

3.4 Relevant Sections Of Ipc In Respect Of Financial Fraud 52

3.5 Miscellaneous Terms Relevant To Fraud 59

Chapter 4: What Is Financial Statement Fraud? Modus Operandi Of Fraud And How To Start Investigation In Respect Of Items Of The Balance Sheet And Profit & Loss Account 65

4.1 What Is Financial Statement Fraud? 65

4.2 Frauds By Journal Entries 66

4.3 Modus Operandi Of Financial Frauds Relating To Main Items Of
   Balance Sheet And How To Investigate 69

4.4 Modus Operandi Of Financial Frauds Relating To Main Items
   Of Profit & Loss Account And How To Investigate 88

4.5 Information Available On The Mca WebsITE 103

Chapter 5: Indicators Of Financial Statement Red Flags – Through Ratio Analysis And Computer-Assisted Software 111

5.1 Ratios 111

5.2 Computer-Assisted Techniques To Detect Red Flags 115

Chapter 6: Banking Fraud Investigation 121

6.1 Steps For Verification From Loan Application To Declaring It As A Fraud 121

6.2 Types Of Different Establishments And Liabilities Of Person . 122

6.3 Types Of Bank Loans 125

6.4 Non-Performing Assets (NPA) 126

6.5 Wilful Default 126

Chapter 7: Criminal Prosecution 131

Chapter 8: Case Studies 135

Chapter 9: Forensic Accounting and Investigation Standards prescribed by ICAI 285

Bibliography/Webliography 289

Glossary 291

Index 299

Table of Case Studies

Name Of The Case and Company Involved	Unit	Reference Page Number
1. Grab & Go Luckin Coffee Inc.	Cheating	135
2. Drive Down Cost & Differ Expenses Sarkar Electronics (Name Changed)	Cheating	137
3. Make Numbers At All Cost Ferro Steel (Name Changed)	Shares Fraud	140
4. Sunita's Entry Vaahan Transportation Services (Name Changed)	Cheating	143
5. Decorating Investor's Dream Universe Décor Limited (Name Changed)	Shares Fraud	146
6. Undisclosed Bank Account Perfect Inc. (Name Changed)	Cheating	149
7. A Super Family Business Super Enterprises (Name Changed)	Cheating	152
8. Ghost Employees Ideal Carriers (Name Changed)	Cheating	155

Name Of The Case and Company Involved	Unit	Reference Page Number
9. Speak Asia Ponzi Scheme Speak Asia Online Limited	Mpid Fraud	158
10. The Story Of India's Biggest Corporate Fraud Satyam Computer Services Ltd.	Cheating	161
11. Nirav Modi Scam Firestar Diamond International, Gitanjali Group	Banking Fraud	165
12. Ricoh India Accounting Fraud Ricoh India Limited	Cheating	169
13. Expensive Cup Of Coffee Café Coffee Day	Banking Fraud	172
14. King Of Good Times Kingfisher Airlines	Banking Fraud	175
15. Rotomac Fraud Case Rotomac Global Pvt. Ltd. (Formerly Known As Rotomac Pen Pvt. Ltd.)	Banking Fraud	179
16. India's Biggest Bank Fraud Abg Shipyard Ltd.	Banking Fraud	182
17. Dishonesty Does Not Give Power Bhushan Power & Steel Ltd.	Banking Fraud	185
18. All That Shine Are Not Diamonds Winsome Diamonds & Jewellery Ltd.	Banking Fraud	188

Name Of The Case and Company Involved	Unit	Reference Page Number
19. In Your Losses Lies Our Success Religare Enterprise Ltd. And Religare Finvest Ltd.	Banking Fraud	192
20. Experience Change Videocon Industries Ltd.- Icici Bank	Banking Fraud	195
21. All That Glitters Is Not Gold Kanishk Gold Pvt. Ltd.	Banking Fraud	199
22. Sandesara Brothers Scam Sterling Biotech Group	Banking Fraud	202
23. Mammoth Fraud Of Rs. 1 Lakh Crores Il&Fs Group	Banking Fraud	204
24. Fraud Through Journal Entries Shiningstar (Name Changed)	Cheating	208
25. Mstc Gold Fraud Mstc	Banking Fraud	211
26. Housing Cheating Matru Habitat Pvt. Ltd. (Name Changed)	Housing Fraud	214
27. Road To Cheating Steve Engineering & Construction Co. Ltd. (Name Changed)	Cheating	216

Name Of The Case and Company Involved	Unit	Reference Page Number
28. Cheating On Issue Of Shares Mgm Finance Ltd. (Name Changed)	Shares Fraud	219
29. Everything For Family Dhanwan Bank (Name Changed)	Cheating	221
30. Vivo Foreign Companies Case Vivo Mobile India Ltd.	Cheating	225
31 Embezzlement From Aiims Sneh Enterprise And Two Staff Members Of Aiims, Delhi	Cheating	228
32 Fashionable Way To Cheat Intimate Fashions India Ltd.	Shares Fraud	231
33. Theft Of Statutory Fund J Sagar Associates (Law Firm)	Cheating	233
34. Quick Getaway Chinese Controlled Companies	Cheating	235
35. Paper Turnover Companies Shaktibhog Foods Ltd.	Banking Fraud	238
36. Merry Go Round Raja Textiles Pvt. Ltd. (Name Changed)	Cheating	241
37. Hand In Glove With Bank Officials Deewan Housing Finance Ltd. (Dhfl)	Banking Fraud	244

Name Of The Case and Company Involved	Unit	Reference Page Number
38. Midas Touch Deputy General Manager Of Godrej Consumer Products Ltd.	Cheating	246
39. Hdil-Pmc Scam Hdil & Pmc Bank	Banking Fraud	248
40. Horizon Is Always Far Zenith Futures Ltd. (Name Changed)	Cheating	251
41. Secret Warehouses Reebok India	Cheating	254
42. Saradha Scam - Ponzi Scheme Saradha Group Of Companies	Mpid Fraud	256
43. Ima Scam - Ponzi Scheme I Monetary Advisory	Mpid Fraud	258
44. Parmalat - An Old Scam - Fraud Through Domestic And Foreign Subsidiaries Parmalat	Banking Fraud	260
45. 1mdb Scandal - Scam At Highest Level By Abusing Position 1malaysia Development Berhad (1mdb)	Cheating	264

Name Of The Case and Company Involved	Unit	Reference Page Number
46. Toshiba Accounting Scandal - Window Dressing Of Accounts Toshiba Corporation, Japan	Cheating	267
47. Crazy Eddie - Ipo Scandal Crazy Eddie	Shares Fraud	270
48. Nsel Scam National Spot Exchange Ltd. (Nsel)	Cheating	273
49. Diversion Of Bank Funds Through Shell Companies For Personal Gain Abc Limited (Names Changed)	Banking Fraud	276
50. Tyco Scandal - Hitting Two Birds With A Single Stone Tyco International	Cheating	282

Chapter 1

Financial Statement Of The Company

The financial statements of the company consist of the following items:

1. **Balance Sheet:** This is a statement of assets and liabilities as of a specific date. It represents the financial position of the company on that particular day. The balance sheet includes all financial transactions that occurred during the year, taking into account the opening balances from past transactions. It is often referred to as the heart of the company's books of accounts. The balance sheet is divided into two sides: assets and liabilities. It also reflects the net worth of the company, which is the total of shareholder's or owner's capital plus reserves and surplus, both of which appear on the liability side of the balance sheet. Traditionally, the balance sheet was prepared in a horizontal form or "T" form.

2. **Profit & Loss Account**: This statement shows the income and expenses of the company for the financial year, which runs from 1st April to 31st March. It provides a summary of the company's financial performance during that period.

3. **Cash Flow Statement:** This statement summarizes the cash and bank funds received and paid by the company throughout the financial year. It helps analyze the company's cash inflows and outflows, providing insights into its liquidity and financial health.

4. **Contingent Liabilities:** These are liabilities that are not definite or crystallized at the end of the year. They depend on the occurrence of certain events, which may or may not happen. Contingent liabilities are disclosed to provide transparency regarding potential obligations that could affect the company's financial position in the future.

5. **Notes to Accounts:** These provide additional information that is not explicitly mentioned in the balance sheet or profit & loss account. They offer further insights and explanations regarding the company's financial statements, ensuring a comprehensive understanding of its financial performance and position.

1.1 What Is A Balance Sheet?

The balance sheet is a statement of assets and liabilities as of a specific date. It represents the financial status of the company on that particular day. The balance sheet is a result of all financial transactions that occurred during the year, including the opening balances from past transactions. It is often considered the cornerstone of the company's accounting records. The balance sheet has two sides: assets and liabilities. Additionally, it reflects the net worth of the company, which is the total of shareholder's or owner's capital plus reserves and surplus, both of which appear on the liability side of the balance sheet. Traditionally, the balance sheet was prepared in a horizontal form or "T" form. T form of the Balance Sheet is shown as under.

Balance Sheet As On ....

Liabilities	Amount (Inr)	Assets	Amount (Inr)
Shareholder's Funds/Net Worth: (Equity)		Fixed Assets (Non-Current Assets)	
Share Capital	Xxx	Property, Plant & Equipment	Xxx
Reserves & Surplus	Xxx	Investments	Xxx
Long Term Borrowings (Non-Current Liabilities)	Xxx	Current Assets, Loans & Advances	Xxx
Current Liabilities & Provisions	Xxx		
Total	**Xxx**	**Total**	**Xxx**

Contingent Liabilities and Notes to Accounts are reflected below the Balance Sheet, and the figures mentioned therein are not included in the Balance Sheet. Recently, the vertical form of the Balance Sheet has become more popular as it provides a clearer understanding of the sources and application of funds. The previously mentioned "T" form of the Balance Sheet can also be represented in the vertical form as shown below:

Balance Sheet As On ....

Particulars	Amount (INR)
Assets:	
Fixed Assets (Non-Current Assets)	
Property, Plant & Equipment	Xxx
Long Term Investments	Xxx
Current Assets	Xxx
Total	**Xxx**
Equity & Liabilities:	
Equity (Shareholders' Fund/Net Worth)	
Share Capital	Xxx
Reserves & Surplus	Xxx
Liabilities	
Non-Current Liabilities	Xxx
Current Liabilities	Xxx
Total	**Xxx**

Let us understand each item of the Balance Sheet

Assets Side

Fixed Assets: Fixed Assets are assets utilized in the business for an extended period and do not get used up within a year. Typically, the lifespan of fixed assets is more than five years. These assets are commonly referred to as Non-Current Assets since they are utilized in the business for more than five years.

Property, Plant & Equipment: Fixed Assets are now classified as Property, Plant, and Equipment, as well as Long-Term Investments. Property, Plant & Equipment can be further categorized into Tangible and Intangible assets.

Tangible Fixed assets are assets that can be physically touched and seen. On the other hand, intangible assets are assets that cannot be seen or touched. Examples of tangible and intangible assets are as follows:

Tangible Fixed Assets	Intangible Assets
Land & Building	Goodwill
Plant & Machinery	Patents
Furniture & Fixtures	Trademarks
Office Equipment	Copyright
Vehicles, Etc.	Intellectual Property

Fixed Asset	Explanation
Land & Building	Land and Building includes factory buildings, office premises, apartments, shops, industrial galas, and other similar structures.
Plant & Machinery	All equipment and machinery used in the production process, whether or not fixed to the earth, are termed as plant and machinery.
Furniture & Fixtures	Furniture & fixtures include all kinds of office and factory furniture and electrical fittings, such as chairs, tables, shelves, bookcases, filing cabinets, etc.
Office Equipment	Office equipment includes computers, printers, photocopiers, laptops, air conditioners, office water coolers, office refrigerators, etc.
Vehicles	Anything used to transport people or materials is categorized as vehicles. Vehicles include motor cars, trucks, tempos, two-wheelers, forklifts, etc.
Goodwill	Goodwill is the value of the reputation built by the company over a period of time, which can be measured in monetary terms. It is considered an intangible asset, and its value is based on the long-standing market presence of the business and its products. The value of goodwill also depends on the company's past profitability and its ability to generate future profits. Different methods are adopted to calculate the value of goodwill, depending on the specific facts of each case.

Patents	A patent is a right granted for an invention. After conducting extensive research and development on a product, a patent is obtained. Patents can be either product patents or process patents. All expenses incurred for research and development, as well as for registering a patent, are capitalized, making the patent an asset. The cost of this asset or patent is amortized or written off over its useful life.
Trademarks	Generally, the logo or a specific image/sign of the company is registered under copyright or trademark. It can be registered under the Trademark Act of 1999. This symbol or design represents the company's product in the market. All expenses incurred for registering a trademark are capitalized and become an asset. The cost of the asset is amortized or written off over its useful life.
Copyright	Copyright is the protection given to a script or a particular work of talent created by an individual using their own intellectual power. It is registered to prevent others from imitating the original work of the author or creator. Copyright provides exclusive rights to the creator or author. The costs or expenses incurred to create copyright are capitalized and amortized (distributed/written off) over its useful life.

Intellectual Property	Collectively, all the aforementioned intangible assets can be referred to as intellectual property (IP). The value of intellectual property is written off over its useful life. The owner of the intellectual property receives a certificate of registration for such property from the relevant authority. However, in the case of goodwill, the documentary evidence can be a valuation report prepared by a registered valuer of the business being acquired.

Long-Term Investments: Investments made by the company for a period of more than one year are classified as Long-Term Investments. They can be either quoted investments (listed on the stock market) or unquoted investments (not listed on the stock market, such as shares of private limited or unlisted public companies). This category also includes all investments in subsidiaries, joint ventures, or associate companies, whether as equity or debt.

Current Assets: Current assets are assets that can be realized or liquidated within one year. In other words, their value can be realized within a short period of time, typically within a year. Examples of current assets include:

Current Asset	Explanation
Inventories (Stock)	Inventories refer to stocks. Stocks can include raw materials, work-in-progress, or finished goods.
Trade Receivables (Debtors)	Trade Receivables are also referred to as sundry debtors. Debtors are customers who owe money to the company for goods or services sold on credit.
Cash & Bank Balances	All cash and bank balances (including fixed deposits) at the end of the financial year are shown here.
Marketable Short-Term Investments	Investments held for a short period of time, with the intention of selling them within a year, are termed as marketable investments.
Short-term Loans & Advances	Loans & Advances given by the company to employees or any other person for a short period of time, i.e., for less than one year, are shown here. Additionally, any additional loans and advances given by the company, other than equity, to its subsidiaries, associates, or any other parties are also included in this category.

Liability Side

Shareholder's Funds/Net Worth

Shareholder's Funds	Explanation
Equity And Preference Share Capital (Paid Up Value Of The Shares Subscribed By Shareholders)	• Share Capital can be of two types: Equity Share Capital or Preference Share Capital. • Equity share capital represents shares that provide ownership rights to the shareholders in proportion to the equity shares held by them. Shareholders with equity shares also have the right to vote at the General Meetings of the Company. • Preference shares, on the other hand, grant holders preferences in terms of dividend payment before the equity shareholders. However, preference shareholders do not have the right to vote at the General Meetings of the Company. Preference shares carry a fixed percentage of dividends, whereas the dividend percentage for equity shareholders is not fixed. • The payment of dividends depends on the profitability of the company as well as the generous policies of the company's management.

	Shareholder's Funds = Total Assets – Total Outside Liabilities Or Shareholder's Funds = Paid Up Value Of Shares + Reserves & Surplus
Past Retained Earnings (General Reserve)	• Retained earnings represent the accumulated profits of the company from previous periods. From the profits after tax (PAT), the company pays dividends to shareholders and transfers funds to other appropriate statutory funds. • After all the aforementioned transfers from PAT, the remaining profit is transferred to Reserves & Surplus, specifically the General Reserve. • The quantum of the general reserve is used to measure the company's net worth and financial strength. A company with a higher general reserve is considered wealthier.
Other Statutory Reserves	• Other statutory reserves are reserves that are created due to certain provisions of the Companies Act or other statutes (laws). Examples of statutory reserves include Capital Reserve, Capital Redemption Reserve, Securities Premium, etc.

	- If equity shares, preference shares, or debentures are issued at a price higher than their face value, the difference between the issue price and face value is transferred to the securities premium account. For example, if the face value of a share is $10 and the shares are issued at $12, then $2 ($12 - $10) will be transferred to the securities premium account.

Long-Term Borrowing: These are funds borrowed by the company for an extended period of time. Generally, these funds are borrowed for the purpose of acquiring fixed assets. They are also referred to as Non-Current Liabilities. Loans are commonly obtained from banks, financial institutions, or the public through the issuance of debentures or deposits. The tenure of long-term borrowings typically ranges from 5 to 10 years or more. Examples of Long-Term Borrowings include Debentures, Term Loans, Public Deposits, Bonds, etc.

Current Liabilities & Provisions: Liabilities that are payable within a period of one year are classified as current liabilities. Examples of current liabilities include:

Current Liabilities	Explanation
Trade Payables (Creditors/ Vendors)	Vendors/Creditors are individuals or entities from whom we have purchased goods or services on credit. They are the parties to whom the company owes payment for goods or services received.
Outstanding Expenses	Outstanding expenses are expenses such as salary, etc., which are not paid on or before the closing date of the Balance Sheet. Generally, these outstanding expenses are paid in the next year after the closing date of the Balance Sheet.
Bank Overdraft/ Cash Credit Facilities	These are the credit facilities availed by the company from banks. In these facilities, the bank allows the company to withdraw more money than its balance in the account. Generally, there is no security offered in the case of overdraft facilities. However, in cash credit facilities, the company offers its inventory and trade receivables as security.

Provisions	• Provisions are created at the year-end. These provisions are recorded in the accounts through journal entries. They represent expected liabilities related to the year-end.
	• Provisions are made to account for expenses for which services have been availed, but invoices have not been received from the vendors by the year-end. The company estimates this liability on an approximate basis and creates a provision for it since it relates to the same year, before the close of the accounting year.
	• These provisions are essentially outstanding expenses, with the only difference being that the exact amount is not known on the last day of the month. Examples include electricity bills, telephone bills, etc.

1.2 What Is a Profit & Loss Account?

A Profit & Loss Account is a statement that shows the profits earned or losses incurred during the year. It is also known as the Revenue Statement. Typically, when income exceeds expenditure, it represents a profit. Therefore, all incomes earned and all expenditures incurred during the financial year are included in the Profit & Loss statement.

The statement of Profit & Loss can be presented in two formats, horizontally and vertically. The horizontal format of the Profit & Loss Account is as follows:

Profit & Loss Account For The Year Ended.......

Expenses	Amount (Inr)	Incomes	Amount (Inr)
To Opening Stock	Xxx	By Sales Xxx	
To Purchases Xxx		(–) Sales Returns (Xx)	Xxx
(–) Purchase Returns (Xx)	Xxx	By Other Income	Xxx
To Carriage Inwards	Xxx	By Job Work Processing Income	Xxx
To Other Factory Exp	Xxx	By Closing Stock	
To Gross Profit C/D	Xxx		
	Xxx		Xxx
To Administrative Expenses	Xxx	By Gross Profit B/D	Xxx
To Selling & Distribution Expenses	Xxx	By Profit On Sale Of Assets	Xxx
To Finance Cost	Xxx	By Profit On Sale Of Investments	Xxx

To Interest On Loan/Debentures	Xxx	By Sundry Balances Written Back	Xxx
To Depreciation	Xxx	By Interest Income	Xxx
To Bad Debts Written Off	Xxx	By Rent Income	Xxx
To Loss On Sale Of Assets	Xxx		
To Loss On Sale Of Investments	Xxx		
To Investments Written Off	Xxx		
To Balances In Subsidiary W/Off	Xxx		
To Sundry Balances W/Off	Xxx		
To Net Profit C/D	Xxx		
Total	**Xxx**	**Total**	**Xxx**
To Income Tax	Xxx	By Op. Balance Of P&L A/C	Xxx
To Transfer To General Reserve	Xxx		
To Transfer To Statutory Reserve	Xxx	By Net Profit B/D	Xxx
To Dividend	Xxx		

To Retained Profit C/D To B/Sheet	Xxx		
Total	**Xxx**	**Total**	**Xxx**

Let us understand each item of the Profit & Loss Account as under

P&L Items	Explanation
Sales (Revenue)	Sales/Revenue includes the sale of goods or services for cash or credit. Sales returns are deducted from the total sales to obtain the figure of net sales. These represent the earnings generated from the core business operations of the company. Debtors are directly associated with credit sales.
Other Income	There can be income from sources other than the core business of the company. Examples of other income include interest income, dividend income, sale of scrap, income from fluctuations in foreign exchange, etc.
Job Work Processing Income	Job work processing refers to work done on behalf of someone else. It means that another party has outsourced job work to our company, and the company earns income from performing that work. This income is generated by utilizing our own surplus manufacturing capacity or infrastructure, including manpower.

Closing Stock	• Closing stock refers to unsold stock, which is a current asset held in the godown or warehouse at the end of the financial year. The value of the closing stock is reflected on the credit side of the Profit & Loss Account. • These are the goods that remain unsold from the purchases made by the company during the year. The verification of this stock is typically conducted by the company and commented upon by the Auditor in their report. • The closing stock is valued at the lower of cost or market value. It includes the value of raw materials, work-in-progress, and finished goods.
Opening Stock	It refers to the goods that were purchased in the previous year but remained unsold. These goods are reflected on the debit side of the Profit & Loss account since they are available for sale in the current year. The closing stock of the previous year should be treated as the opening stock of the current year.
Purchases	Purchases represent goods acquired during the year for the purpose of sale, whether made on cash or credit. Generally, if there are any purchase returns, they are deducted from the total figure of Purchases. Creditors are directly associated with credit purchases.

Carriage Inward	It is the expense incurred for the loading and unloading of purchased goods. This expense is considered a direct expense and is incurred at the factory or warehouse.
Other Factory Overheads	Overheads refer to the allocation of general expenses incurred, such as rent of warehouse/factory premises, factory insurance premiums, supervisor salaries, etc. In the case of manufacturing concerns, other factory overheads are debited to the Profit & Loss Account to calculate the gross profit.
Gross Profit	Gross profit is calculated by subtracting the cost of goods sold from sales. The cost of goods sold includes not only the value of purchases but also direct expenditures related to purchases or manufacturing the product. Additionally, the value of opening stock is added, and the closing stock is deducted from the value of purchases to arrive at the figure of the cost of sales.

Gross Profit = Net Sales + Closing Stock − Opening Stock - Net Purchases - Carriage Inwards - Factory Expenses/Overheads The gross profit obtained is then transferred to the credit side of the Profit & Loss Account. |
| **Profit On Sale Of Assets** | When fixed assets are sold during the year at a price higher than their carrying amount in the balance sheet, a profit is realized. This profit is credited to the Profit & Loss account. |

Profit On Sale Of Investments	When investments are sold during the year at a price higher than their cost, the profit is credited to the Profit & Loss Account.
Sundry Balances Written Back	Creditors are individuals or entities to whom payment is owed for goods or services provided. If the company is no longer required to pay these creditors due to various reasons, they are written back and reflected as income since the liability of the company is no longer applicable.
Interest Income	Interest is the income generated from loans and advances given, as well as interest earned on investments. For example, it includes interest on fixed deposits and interest on loans given.
Rent Income	When a company rents out its vacant or spare property, it earns rental income.
Administrative Expenses	Administrative expenses are the expenses incurred by a company for its day-to-day operations. These expenditures are necessary to run the daily affairs of the company and are typically of a fixed nature. Examples of administrative expenses include employee benefit expenses such as salaries, staff welfare expenses, contributions to PF, printing and stationery, rent, legal expenses, insurance, etc.

Selling & Distribution Expenses	All costs incurred by the company related to marketing, such as advertising, website maintenance, distribution costs including logistics and insurance, and selling expenses like sales commissions and sales promotion expenses, are collectively referred to as Selling & Distribution expenses.
Finance Cost	These expenses can also be referred to as financing costs, which include interest paid/payable on loans and debentures, loan processing fees, bank charges, etc.
Depreciation	Depreciation is the gradual but permanent decrease in the value of a fixed asset. It represents the wear and tear of the asset while being used during the year. Depreciation is considered a non-cash expenditure. It is charged through a journal entry, thereby reducing the value of the fixed asset. Depreciation is recorded in the Profit & Loss Account to distribute the cost of the asset over its useful life.
Bad Debts written off	Bad debts are the amounts written off during the year against sundry debtors. If the money is no longer recoverable from the debtors due to their insolvency or other reasons, it is written off during the year.

Loss on Sale of Assets	When a fixed asset is sold during the year, and the selling price is less than the carrying cost of the asset, it is referred to as a loss on the sale of the asset.
Loss on Sale of Investments	If investments are sold during the year at a price lower than the cost, a loss on the sale of the investment is incurred.
Investments Written off	Investments are made by the company with the intention of earning profits or income. However, sometimes these investments turn bad due to poor performance, repeated losses, or a decline in the net worth of the company in which the investments are made. In such cases, these investments need to be written off as their market value becomes zero. Since this reduction in the value of the investment represents a loss for us, it appears on the debit side of the Profit & Loss Account.
Balances in Subsidiaries written off	Subsidiary companies are companies in which the parent company or holding company holds more than 50% of the shares. In cases where the subsidiary company's net worth is eroded or it incurs significant losses, the balance in the subsidiary is written off by the company. This results in a loss for the company as there is a reduction in the value of the asset (investment in the subsidiary).

Net Profit	Net profit is the amount of profit earned by the business after deducting all expenses. Net Profit = Income earned during the year − Expenditure incurred during the year. From the net profit earned during the year, the amount of dividend declared or the amount transferred to statutory reserves is deducted. The remaining balance of the net profit is transferred to the General Reserve.
Income Tax	Income tax is paid on the net profit earned by the company during the year. Income tax paid by the company is not considered an expense but rather an appropriation of profit. Therefore, the tax on income is debited to the Profit & Loss Appropriation Account before the amount is transferred to the General Reserve.
Transfer to Statutory Reserve	As per the requirements of any statute or the Companies Act; companies are obligated to transfer funds to statutory reserves. Examples of such reserves include the debenture redemption fund, investment allowance reserve, etc.
Dividend	Dividend is paid to the shareholders from the surplus, which is the net profits of the company reduced by tax payments. It is a distribution of profits to the shareholders from the earnings of the company. Therefore, it is considered an appropriation of profit.

Transfer to General Reserve	General Reserve represents the remaining profit from the net profit earned during the year after accounting for all appropriations, such as dividend payments and income tax. The balance remaining after tax and dividend payments are made is transferred to the General Reserve.

1.3 What Are Cash Flow Statement And Fund Flow Statements?

A Cash flow statement is a statement prepared by the company to reflect the movement of funds during the year. It is the inflow and outflow of cash during the year. This statement has three types of Cash flows:

i. **Cash From Operating Activities:** Cash movements of activities relating to core business (operating) activities.

ii. **Cash From Investing Activities:** Cash movements of activities relating to investments made, whether in other companies or purchase/sale of fixed assets, etc.

iii. **Cash From Financing Activities** - Cash movements of activities relating to borrowing funds, raising capital, etc.

Sample Cash Flow Statement

	Particulars	INR	INR
I.	Cash Flows from Operating Activities (A)		xxx
II.	Cash Flows from Investing Activities (B)		xxx
III.	Cash Flows from Financing Activities (C)		xxx
	Net Cash Generated during the Year (D=A+B+C)	xxx	
	Add: Cash & Cash Equivalents at the beginning of the year (E)	xxx	
	Cash & Cash Equivalents at the end of the year (F= D+E)		xxx

Fund Flow Statement

A funds flow statement is prepared to analyze changes in the financial position between the two Balance Sheet dates. It consists of two sides: Sources and Applications. The Sources side shows where the money has come into the business, and the Applications side shows where the funds are spent or applied. The funds' flow statement also takes into account the changes in working capital. In other words, the funds' flow statement shows the inflow and outflow of funds of the business during the two Balance Sheet dates.

Sources of Funds	Amount	Application of Funds	Amount
Capital Introduced/ Issue of shares	xxx	Purchase of Fixed Assets	xxx
Funds Borrowed as loans	xxx	Purchase of Investments	xxx
Sale of Fixed Assets	xxx	Repayment of Loans	xxx
Funds From Operations (Difference in Reserves)	xxx	Dividends Paid	xxx
Decrease in Working Capital	xxx	Increase in Working Capital	xxx
	XXX		XXX

This statement shows the sources (whether long-term or short-term) of funds and their applications (long-term or short-term). A decrease in working capital signifies a shortage of long-term sources to finance long-term assets.

In this digital era, all accounting is conducted in a digital mode using software. All accounting software or ERP software automatically prepares the fund flow statement with just one click for any required period.

There are money trail software available that shows the sources and applications of money from bank statements. An example of a money trail is provided on the next page.

Combined Fund Flow of AB Limited and CD Limited (Listed Companies) (Preferential Equity) (FY 20-21)

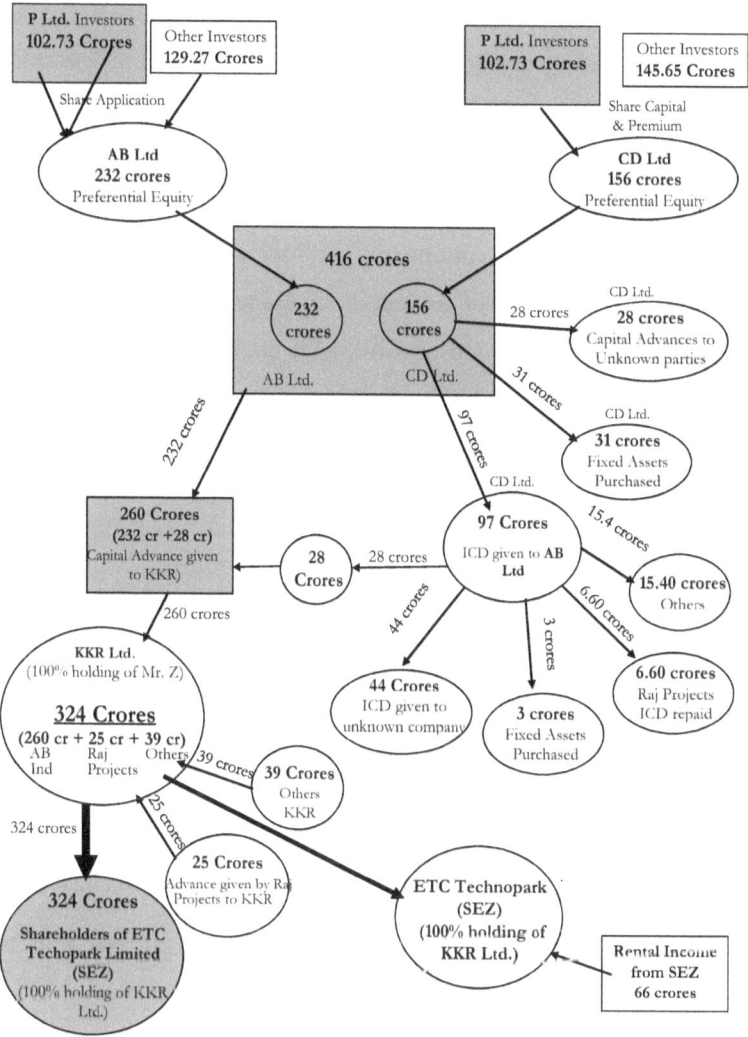

1.4 Contingent Liabilities

Contingent Liability is a liability that is not definite or crystallized at the end of the year. This is because it depends on a future event that may or may not occur. Consequently, there is no present obligation to pay for these liabilities. Examples of contingent liabilities include a pending court suit with an uncertain outcome for the company or a disputed amount of tax for which an appeal is pending in court. The nature and amount of contingent liabilities are usually mentioned below the Balance Sheet as footnotes. Many times, if a company reports a significant value of contingent liabilities, it may indicate poor financial health. Additionally, it provides an early indication of potential liabilities that the company may incur in the future.

1.5 What Are Notes To Accounts?

Notes to Accounts provide detailed information about certain items in the financial statements that are not specifically disclosed in them. They also disclose certain transactions that do not appear on the Balance Sheet. Information that cannot be included in the Balance Sheet but has a significant impact on the company's position is presented as notes to accounts. Some instances of items mentioned in the notes to accounts of companies' financial statements include

1. Accounting policies and procedures used during the year to prepare financial statements.

2. Changes in accounting policies and procedures, such as a change in the method of valuing stock and its impact on the Profit & Loss during the year.

3. All disclosures related to accounting standards adopted by the company during the year, etc.

Chapter 2

Auditor's & Director's Roles and Responsibilities

2.1 Appointment Of Auditors (Section 139 Of Companies Act, 2013)

a. The first auditors are appointed by the Board of Directors within 30 days of incorporation. If the Board of Directors fails to appoint an auditor within 90 days of incorporation, the auditors can be appointed by the Shareholders in an extraordinary general meeting.

b. During the first Annual General Meeting, the Shareholders appoint the auditors, and they hold office for a period of five years. In the case of listed companies, the auditor firm can hold office for two consecutive terms, totaling ten years. However, an individual auditor of a listed company can hold office only for a period of five years, which is one term. After completing their term, there is a cooling-off period of five years before they can be re-appointed.

c. In the event of a casual vacancy due to sudden death, insanity, or insolvency of the auditor, the shareholders appoint new auditors within three months of such vacancy, and they hold office until the next Annual General Meeting.

For Government Companies, auditors are appointed by the Comptroller & Auditor General of India (CAG).

Persons not eligible for appointment as an auditor of the company are

1. A body corporate (LLP can be appointed as auditors)

2. Officers/employees of the company

3. Persons having a business relationship with the company

4. A person whose relative is a director or Key Managerial Personnel (KMP) of the company

5. Individuals holding appointments as auditors in 20 or more companies (The limit excludes unlisted companies having paid-up share capital of less than Rs. 100 crores)

6. Persons convicted by a court, and 10 years have not elapsed from the verdict

7. A person engaged in providing any other service to the company (except CA services)

8. A person who, or whose relative/partner:

- Holds any security in the company (relatives can hold up to Face value Rs. 1 Lakh)

- Is indebted to the company for more than Rs. 5 Lakh

- Has given a guarantee for a third party to the company for Rs. 1 Lakh or more.

The above disqualifications are established to ensure that auditors act independently without coming under the influence of the management. They are expected to be unbiased, independent, and responsible while providing reports to the shareholders of the company.

2.2 Auditors' Report under CARO

The Ministry of Corporate Affairs (MCA) issued the Companies (Auditor's Report) Order, commonly known as CARO. CARO covers reporting by auditors on 21 points. The main points of reporting under CARO are as follows:

Sr No	Point in CARO	Details
1	**Maintaining records of Property, Plant, Equipment, and intangible assets**	• Whether the company has maintained proper records of fixed assets (tangible and intangible), including quantitative details.

		• Whether the title deeds of the fixed assets are in the name of the company (except for leased assets). The auditor is required to verify the copy of the invoice, along with the delivery challan and installation report for fixed assets purchased by the company.
		• Whether the fixed assets have been physically verified by the management or not.
		• If the company has revalued assets during the year, whether the value is in accordance with the valuation report.
		• Whether any proceedings have been initiated against the company for holding any benami property.
2	**Physical Verification of Inventories**	• Whether the physical verification of inventory has been conducted by the management and if any discrepancies of more than 10% have been noticed, whether they are properly dealt with in the books of accounts.

		• In case the company has availed working capital loans in excess of Rs. 5 crores or more on the security of current assets, whether the quarterly reports filed by the company to such institutions are in agreement with the books of accounts or not.
3	**Repayment of investments, guarantee, security, and loans granted by the Company**	• This reporting by the auditor pertains to loans given during the year and is one of the crucial clauses for investigation as it deals with potential diversion or siphoning off of funds. • The auditor is required to show the aggregate amount of loans given during the year and outstanding at the end of the year separately for subsidiaries, associates, joint ventures, and outsiders. • Additionally, the auditor needs to verify whether interest/principal amounts are being repaid regularly by these parties. • Furthermore, the auditor should report on the total amount overdue for more than 90 days.

		• Finally, the auditor must check if the company has granted any loans without specifying the repayment period. If such loans exist, detailed information about them needs to be reported.
4	**Default in repayment of loans or other borrowings**	• Whether the company has defaulted in the principal and interest repayment of any loans borrowed, and if so, details need to be reported. • Whether the company has been declared as a wilful defaulter by any bank or financial institution. • Whether the loans are used for the purpose for which they were granted. If not, the amount of diversion needs to be reported. • Whether any loan has been taken to meet the obligations of subsidiaries, associates, joint ventures, etc. If yes, details need to be reported.

5	**Disclosure of transactions not recorded in the books**	• Whether any transactions not recorded in books of accounts are disclosed as income under the Income Tax Act; if yes, whether the previously undisclosed transactions were dealt with properly in the books of accounts later.
6	**Money raised by IPO, FPO & preferential allotment/ private placement of shares or convertible debentures**	• Whether any money raised by IPO, FPO, Preferential allotment, or convertible debentures are applied towards the purposes for which they were raised. If not, the details need to be reported. • In other words, if there is any diversion of money to subsidiaries and associates, it is required to be reported under this item.
7	**Fraud reporting**	• Whether any fraud has been noticed or reported. If yes, the nature and amount involved should be reported.

		• During the course of the audit, if the auditor finds material discrepancies with regard to fixed assets, stocks, debtors, creditors, diversion of funds, diversion of income, unauthorized payments, payments unrelated to the activities of the company, diversion of funds to directors and their relatives, or suppression of income, it is the duty of the auditor to report the same under this head. The auditor should also advise conducting a special audit/forensic audit to investigate the deficiencies or prima facie fraudulent practices.
8	**Transactions with the related parties (sections 177 and 188)**	• This reporting by the auditor pertains to transactions with related parties during the year and is one of the crucial clauses for investigation as it deals with potential diversion or siphoning off of funds. • Diversion of funds to subsidiaries can occur through various means, such as diversion of income, giving advances, allotting contracts, making fake payments against fake invoices, opening foreign subsidiaries, making inflated purchases, and utilizing manpower, as well as through under-invoicing.

8		• The auditor needs to check whether a board resolution has been passed to approve all related party transactions.
		• Additionally, the auditor should verify whether related party transactions that are not in the ordinary course of business or not at arm's length and transactions above the threshold limits are approved by shareholders in the general meeting.
9	**Non-cash transactions with directors**	• Non-cash transactions refer to the benefits passed on to the directors indirectly by making personal use of company assets.
		• For instance, items such as computers, televisions, air conditioners, etc., are billed to the company but taken by the directors for their personal use.

- The auditor is required to report such indirect benefits in their report. Often, significant assets purchased in the company's name are diverted to the directors for their personal and family use, such as high-value cars purchased by the company but utilized by the director's family. These benefits, known as perquisites or benefits in kind, need to be reported as this diversion is part of the fraud perpetrated by the management.

2.3 Qualified Audit Report

A Qualified audit report is issued by an auditor when they find material discrepancies and the statement of accounts not being true and fair regarding certain transactions. However, an auditor might provide a clean report for certain areas and issue a qualified report for others. This means that there may be material misstatements in the financial statements, but they only affect specific areas. As a result, auditors have to qualify the report with regard to the area that does not reflect a true and fair view of the financial statements.

Some Examples Of Qualified Report

a. The Company has accumulated losses, and its net worth has been fully eroded. The Company incurred a net cash loss during the year ended March 31, 2021, as well as in previous years. Additionally, the Company's current liabilities exceeded its current assets as of March 31, 2021. These conditions indicate the existence of a material uncertainty that may cast significant doubt on the Company's ability to continue as a going concern. However, the standalone financial statements of the Company have been prepared on a going concern basis.

b. The Company has invested Rs. 50 Crore in ABC WLL, Qatar, through its subsidiary. ABC WLL has been incurring losses, leading to the erosion of its net worth due to continuing losses. No provision for diminution in the value of the investment is made. As a result, we are unable to comment on the same and ascertain its impact, if any, on the net loss for the year ended March 31, 2021, the carrying value of the investment, and other equity as of March 31, 2021, with respect to the above matters.

2.4 Criminal Liability Of Auditors

Acts	Section Under Companies Act 2013
Non-Compliance by Auditor	Under Section 143 & 145, if the auditor fails to comply with regard to making his report, signing, or authorization of any document, and engages in willful neglect on his part, he shall be punishable with imprisonment of up to one year or with a fine not less than ₹25,000, extendable to ₹5,00,000.

Failure to assist investigation	Section 217(6): When the Central Government appoints an Inspector to investigate the affairs of the company, it becomes the duty of the auditor to produce all books and documents and provide assistance to the inspectors. If the auditor fails to do so, he shall be punished with imprisonment of up to one year and with a fine of up to ₹1,00,000.
Liabilities for Professional Misconduct	The Chartered Accountant Act 1949 mentions a number of acts and omissions that constitute professional misconduct in relation to audit practice. If the council of ICAI finds an auditor guilty of professional misconduct, the auditor's name may be removed for a period of five years or more.

Sections Related To Directors, Their Roles, And Criminal Liabilities

2.5 Sections Of Companies Act, 2013 Related To Directors

Section	Content
149(1)	Minimum/Maximum number of Directors in a company
165	Number of Directorships
149(3)	At least one Director to be Resident in India – 182 days stay in India
132	Appointment of Directors

159	Punishment (contravening section 152/155/156)
161(1)	Appointment of Additional Directors
161(2)	Appointment of Alternate Directors
161(3)	Appointment of Directors by Nomination
164	Disqualifications for Appointment of Directors
166	Duties of Directors
167	Vacation of Office of Director
169	Removal of Directors
170(1) & Rule 17	Register of KMP

2.6 Role Of Directors

a. Subject to the provisions of this Act, a director of a company shall act in accordance with the articles of the company.

b. A director of a company shall act in good faith to promote the objects of the company for the benefit of its members as a whole and in the best interests of the company, its employees, the shareholders, the community, and for the protection of the environment.

c. A director of a company shall exercise their duties with due and reasonable care, skill, and diligence, and they shall exercise independent judgment.

d. A director of a company shall not be involved in a situation in which they may have a direct or indirect interest that conflicts, or possibly may conflict, with the interest of the company.

e. A director of a company shall not achieve or attempt to achieve any undue gain or advantage either for themselves or for their relatives, partners, or associates. If such a director is found guilty of making any undue gain, they shall be liable to pay an amount equal to that gain to the company.

f. A director of a company shall not assign their office, and any assignment so made shall be void.

g. If a director of the company contravenes the provisions of this section, such director shall be punishable with a fine which shall not be less than INR 1 Lakh but which may extend to INR 5 Lakh.

2.7 Criminal Liability Of Directors

Criminal liability consists of two main elements:

1. The guilty Act, which is otherwise known as actus reus.

2. The guilty mind, also known as Mens Rea.

Since a company is an artificial entity, it cannot have a guilty mind or Mens Rea to commit a criminal offense.

However, when a criminal offense committed by a company involves Mens Rea, we can establish that the offense was committed by the person acting on behalf of the company. Therefore, the person who acts on behalf of the company, i.e., the director of the company, would be held liable since their actions perpetrated the offense on behalf of the company.

Lifting Of Corporate Veil

a. The doctrine of lifting the corporate veil means disregarding the corporate nature of the body of individuals incorporated as a company. A company is a juristic person, but in reality, it is a group of people who are the beneficial owners of the property of the corporate body. Being an artificial person, the company cannot act on its own; it can only act through natural persons. The doctrine of lifting the veil can be understood as the process of identifying the company with its members.

b. The need for the Doctrine of Lifting the Corporate Veil arises when unscrupulous individuals use the corporate veil as an instrument to conceal fraud in the company's affairs. Therefore, it becomes essential for the legislature and the courts to develop and apply the doctrine of lifting the corporate veil to uncover the individuals behind the company, who are the actual beneficiaries of the corporate body.

Section of the Companies Act, 2013	Content	Punishment
34	Untrue Statement In lieu of Prospectus	Imprisonment upto two years or fine of Rs. 5000 or both
53	Prohibition on issue of shares at discount	Fine between Rs. 1 lakh to Rs. 5 lakhs

68	Buying back of shares	Imprisonment upto three years or fine of Rs. 1 Lakh or both
92	Annual returns in prescribed form	Imprisonment upto six months or fine of Rs. 50,000 to Rs. 5 lakhs or both
118	Duty to preserve minutes of Company	Imprisonment upto 2 years or fine of Rs. 25,000 to Rs. 1 Lakh or both
128	Maintenance of Proper books of Accounts of Company	Imprisonment upto 1 year or fine of Rs. 50,000 to Rs. 5 lakhs or both

Director's Liabilities can be Classified into the following

a. Breach of fiduciary duty – Directors hold the office in trust and must exercise their powers in the best interest of the company.

b. Ultra vires Act – A director acts beyond the powers sanctioned under the Companies Act, Memorandum, and Articles of Association.

c. Negligence – Refers to a failure to exercise care and caution. However, an error of judgment cannot be construed as negligence.

d. Mala fide Acts – Directors are liable for breach of trust if found misusing their powers with malicious intent.

2.8 Appointment Of Foreign National As Director In Indian Company

a. Foreign individuals or non-resident Indians residing outside of India can become executives or directors of Indian companies, whether publicly listed, unlisted, or private, by complying with the rules given in Part 1 of Schedule V of the Companies Act, 2013, along with the Companies (Appointment and Qualifications of Directors) Rules, 2014.

b. Additionally, foreign nationals or non-resident Indians can also be appointed as Whole Time Directors (WTD) or Managing Directors (MD), subject to compliance with one of the conditions in Part 1 of Schedule V. The Act states that a person appointed as a whole-time director or managing director should be a resident of India.

c. For the purpose of Schedule V, a resident in India includes a person who has been staying in India for a continuous period of not less than twelve months immediately preceding the date of their appointment as a managerial person and who has come to stay in India for taking up employment or carrying on a business or vacation.

d. However, this condition shall not apply to companies in Special Economic Zones as notified by the Department of Commerce from time to time. Non-resident individuals seeking appointment as whole-time directors or managing directors shall enter India only after obtaining a proper Employment Visa from the concerned Indian mission abroad. To this effect, such persons shall be required to furnish, along with the visa application form, the profile of the company, the principal employer, and the terms and conditions of their appointment.

e. In case the conditions under Schedule V are not satisfied, prior permission from the Central Government must be obtained through the e-form MR-2 for the appointment as a Whole-time director or Managing Director.

Requirements Under FEMA Act, 1999

a. A foreign national being appointed as a director in an Indian concern receives the same privileges as an Indian national, including adequate remuneration, commissions, and sitting fees.

b. In addition to these, a foreign national is required to comply with the provisions of the FEMA Act, 1999.

c. Foreign nationals who are to be appointed as directors must hold a valid Indian employment visa.

d. They can hold a foreign currency account in an authorized bank stationed outside India, where they can transfer their remuneration received for acting as a director in an Indian company.

e. An Indian company appointing a foreign director must make appropriate arrangements for remunerating them, such as making applications to the respective dealers. An undertaking certificate must be enclosed along with a statement regarding the payment of income tax.

2.9 Fiduciary Duty Of Directors

a. Any relationship involving trust is a fiduciary relationship. This means that a director has to act bona fide in the best interest of the company.

b. These duties can be understood as derived from the law of trust and agency, where shareholders impose fiduciary duties on the directors, and the directors are mandated to fulfill duties of skill, care, and diligence.

Case Law - Globe Motors Vs. Mehta Teja Singh (1984) 55 Com Cases 445 (Del)

- In this case, the company and its distributors (respondent) entered into two agreements for the sales and marketing of the company's product, which is steel. The board of directors ratified these agreements, which benefited 6 out of the total 13 directors. The issue arose later during the process of winding up, and the official liquidator of the company contended for rescinding these agreements in the interest of the company.

- The court held that the terms of the agreements were detrimental to the interest of the company and, thus, held them to be void. The ratio of the case was that the directors' duty is to act for the benefit of the company and must disregard their private interests. The case set a strong precedent to ensure the 'fiduciary duties' of directors, further enhanced under section 184 of the Act.

2.10 Independent Directors – Appointment, Roles, And Criminal Liabilities

An independent director is a non-executive director of a company who assists the company in improving corporate credibility and governance standards. He or she does not have any relationship with the company that may influence the independence of their judgment. Independent directors act as mentors to the company.

According to Section 149 of the Companies Act 2013, every listed public company should appoint at least one-third of its directors as independent directors. In the case of the following classes of public companies, at least two independent directors need to be appointed:

- Paid-up share capital of Rs. 10 crores or more.

- Turnover of Rs. 100 crores or more.

- Aggregate outstanding loans, debentures, and deposits of Rs. 50 crores or more.

Note:

a. The amounts, as per the latest audited financial statements, should be taken into account for calculating the above criteria.

b. Joint ventures, wholly-owned subsidiaries, or dormant companies are not required to appoint independent directors, even if they meet all the above criteria.

Role Of Independent Directors

- An independent director should provide an independent judgment on any Board matter.

- They should also prevent the management from making decisions that go against the interests of the shareholders.

- Their responsibilities include ensuring that there are no fraudulent or unethical practices occurring within the company and that the company has a robust and functional vigil mechanism.

- Additionally, independent directors should ensure that the company's policies are not violated.

- They are also responsible for reviewing and monitoring the auditor's independence, performance, and effectiveness of the audit process.

- Furthermore, independent directors play a crucial role in formulating a succession plan to ensure corporate governance, stability, and the long-term sustainability of the business.

The criminal liabilities of independent directors are the same as the criminal liabilities of the directors.

Chapter 3
Forensic Accounting & Auditing

3.1 What Is Forensic?

According to the Oxford Dictionary, "Forensic" means scientific tests or techniques used in connection with the detection of crime. Therefore, the use of scientific techniques for crime detection is considered forensic. Similarly, utilizing various techniques and advanced technology/methodology to analyze financial data and information is also referred to as financial forensics.

3.2 What Is Forensic Auditing?

Forensic Auditing involves data mining, data analysis, and the identification of crucial data for establishing financial crime under the relevant sections of the Indian Penal Code. In other words, it is a technique used to analyze and present financial data or information from a company's financial records in a manner acceptable to a court of law. Forensic Auditing focuses on investigating financial fraud through in-depth analysis of financial statements. As such, forensic accountants serve as auditors and fraud investigators.

3.3 What Is Fraud?

The term 'fraud' is not explicitly defined in the Indian Penal Code (IPC); instead, it explains what constitutes fraudulent actions. Fraudulent activities are covered under section 25 of the IPC, which defines the term 'fraudulently' as follows: "A person is said to do a thing fraudulently if he does it with intent to defraud but not otherwise." In essence, any act committed with the intent to cheat, obtain an undeserved benefit or advantage or knowingly deny someone their entitled benefit is considered fraud.

According to the explanation under section 447 of the Companies Act, 2013, fraud is described as any act, omission, concealment of facts, or abuse of position committed by a person or in connivance with another person, with the intent to deceive, gain undue advantage, or harm the interests of the company, its shareholders, creditors, or any other person, whether or not there is any wrongful gain or wrongful loss.

3.4 Relevant Sections Of Ipc In Respect Of Financial Fraud

Section	Explanation
Section 24 Dishonestly	Whoever does anything with the intention of causing wrongful gain to one person or wrongful loss to another person is said to do that thing 'dishonestly.'

	Wrongful gain refers to the acquisition of property through unlawful means to which the person gaining it is not legally entitled.	
	Wrongful loss, on the other hand, pertains to the deprivation of property through unlawful means to which the person losing it is legally entitled.	
Section 25 Fraudulently	A person is said to do a thing fraudulently if he does that thing with the intent to defraud but not otherwise.	
Section 34 Punishment For Criminal Act Done By Several Persons	A criminal act done by several persons in furtherance of the common intention of all makes each of those persons liable for that act in the same manner as if it was done by him alone. This section enables the purpose of fixing criminal liability for each person involved in the crime.	
	Punishment under section 34 is in accordance with the punishments provided for the crimes committed as per the Indian Penal Code. This section is always read in conjunction with other substantive sections of the IPC.	
Section 120B Punishment For Criminal Conspiracy	1. Whoever is a party to a criminal conspiracy to commit an offense punishable with death, imprisonment for life, or rigorous imprisonment for a term of two years or more shall, where no express provision is made in this Code for the punishment of such a conspiracy, be punished in the same manner as if he had abetted such offense.	

	2. Whoever is a party to a criminal conspiracy other than a criminal conspiracy to commit an offense punishable as aforesaid shall be punished with imprisonment of either description for a term not exceeding six months, or with a fine, or with both.
Section 206 Fraudulent Removal Or Concealment Of Property	Fraudulent removal or concealment of property to prevent its seizure as forfeited or in execution is punishable. The punishment under this section shall be imprisonment of either description for a term which may extend to two years, or with a fine, or with both.
Section 403 Dishonest Dealing In Property	When a person dishonestly misappropriates or uses the property of another person to satisfy his own purpose or capitalize it for one's own use, they have committed the offense of criminal misappropriation. The punishment under this section shall be imprisonment of either description for a term which may extend to two years, or with a fine, or with both.

| Section 405 & 406

Criminal Breach Of Trust And Its Punishment | Whoever, being in any manner entrusted with property or with any dominion over property, dishonestly misappropriates or converts it to his own use, or dishonestly uses or disposes of that property in violation of any direction of law prescribing the mode in which such trust is to be discharged, or of any legal contract, express or implied, which he has made concerning the discharge of such trust, or willfully allows any other person to do so, commits a criminal breach of trust.

Whoever commits a criminal breach of trust shall be punished with imprisonment of either description for a term which may extend to three years or with a fine or with both. |
|---|---|
| Section 409

Criminal Breach Of Trust By Public Servant, Banker, Merchant Or Agent | Whoever, being in any manner entrusted with property or having any dominion over the property in his capacity as a public servant or in the course of his business as a banker, merchant, factor, broker, attorney, or agent, commits a criminal breach of trust in respect of that property, shall be punished with imprisonment for life or with imprisonment of either description for a term which may extend to ten years, and shall also be liable to a fine. |

Section 410 & 411 Possessing Stolen Property	A property whose possession has been transferred by theft, extortion, or robbery and which has been criminally misappropriated or in respect of which a criminal breach of trust has been committed is considered as "stolen property," regardless of whether the transfer, misappropriation, or breach of trust occurred within or outside India. Whoever dishonestly receives or retains any stolen property, knowing or having reason to believe it to be stolen property, shall be punished with imprisonment of either description for a term which may extend to three years, with a fine, or with both.
Section 420 Cheating	Cheating and dishonestly inducing the delivery of property. Whoever cheats and thereby dishonestly induces the person deceived to deliver any property to any person, or to make, alter, or destroy the whole or any part of a valuable security, or anything which is signed or sealed, and which is capable of being converted into a valuable security, shall be punished with imprisonment of either description for a term which may extend to seven years, and shall also be liable to a fine.

Section 463 & 465 Forgery And Its Punishment	Whoever makes any false document or false electronic record, or any part of a document or electronic record, with the intent to cause damage or injury to the public or to any person, or to support any claim or title, or to cause any person to part with property, or to enter into any express or implied contract, or with the intent to commit fraud or facilitate fraud, commits forgery. Whoever commits forgery shall be punished with imprisonment of either description for a term which may extend to two years, with a fine, or with both.
Section 464 Making A False Document	Whoever dishonestly or fraudulently engages in the falsification or alteration of a document, electronic record, or electronic signature is said to make a false document. Whoever deals in making such false documents shall be punished with imprisonment of either description for a term which may extend to two years, with a fine, or with both (under section 465).

| Section 467
Forgery Of Valuable Security, Will, Etc.	Whoever forges a document which purports to be a valuable security or a will, or an authority to adopt a son, or which purports to give authority to any person to make or transfer any valuable security, or to receive the principal, interest, or dividends thereon, or to receive or deliver any money, movable property, or valuable security, or any document purporting to be an acquittance or receipt acknowledging the payment of money, or an acquittance or receipt for the delivery of any movable property or valuable security, shall be punished with imprisonment for life, or with imprisonment of either description for a term which may extend to ten years, and shall also be liable to a fine.
Section 471
Using As Genuine A Forged Document Or Electronic Record	Whoever fraudulently or dishonestly uses as genuine any document or electronic record which he knows or has reason to believe to be a forged document or electronic record shall be punished in the same manner as if he had forged such document or electronic record, i.e., imprisonment of either description for a term which may extend to two years, or with a fine, or with both.

Section	Whoever, being a clerk, officer, or servant, or employed or acting in the capacity of a clerk, officer, or servant, willfully and with intent to defraud, destroys, alters, mutilates, or falsifies any book, electronic record, paper, writing, valuable security, or account which belongs to or is in the possession of his employer, or has been received by him for or on behalf of his employer, or willfully and with intent to defraud, makes or abets the making of any false entry in, or omits or alters or abets the omission or alteration of any material particular from or in any such book, electronic record, paper, writing, valuable security, or account, shall be punished with imprisonment of either description for a term which may extend to seven years, or with a fine, or with both.
477A Falsification Of Accounts	

3.5 Miscellaneous Terms Relevant To Fraud

3.5.1 What Is Money Laundering?

Money laundering is a process in which illegally obtained money is introduced by criminals into the legal channel by placement, layering, and integration to make it look legal. Illegally obtained money can be introduced into official channels by showing sales in cash-intensive businesses, investing in overseas shell companies, breaking the money into smaller tranches, and using different accounts to launder the same. Additionally, criminals may invest in luxurious commodities like diamonds, gold, etc., which can be moved easily from one place to another. Thus, the money is placed into official channels, layered in many accounts, and later integrated to complete the laundering process. It is a way to transform illegal money into clean, seemingly legitimate funds.

3.5.2 Platform Of Fraud Through Subsidiary, Step-Down Subsidiaries & Associate Companies

Subsidiary Company

"Subsidiary company" or "subsidiary," in relation to any other company (that is to say, the holding company), means a company in which the holding company:

a. Controls the composition of the Board of Directors (2/3rd) (Common Directors); or

b. Exercises or controls more than one-half of the total voting power (50%) either on its own or together with one or more of its subsidiary companies (Common Shareholders).

The subsidiary company includes the Subsidiary of the Subsidiary

Associate Company

a. "Associate company," in relation to another company, means a company in which that other company has a significant influence but is not a subsidiary company of the company having such influence, and includes a joint venture company.

b. The expression "significant influence" means control of at least 20% of the total voting power or control of or participation in business decisions under an agreement.

c. If an entity/person owns more than 20% of the total share capital of, let's say, 'Company D,' or if an entity or a person has the right to appoint a majority of the directors in Company D through any agreement (shareholders agreement or others), or if there exists any agreement that allows the entity/person to control key decisions of Company D, then such entity/person is considered an associated party to Company D.

The above-mentioned subsidiary companies, associates, and sub-subsidiaries are called sister concerns.

The concept of Subsidiary, Associate, Step-Down Subsidiary can be explained further as follows:

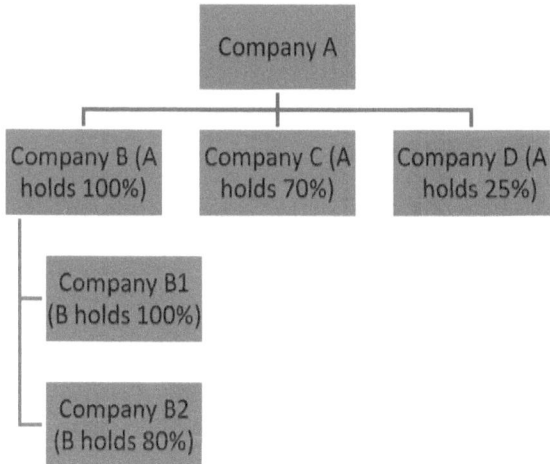

- Company A is holding Company of B and C

- Company B is a fully owned subsidiary of A

- Company C is a partially owned subsidiary of A

- Company D is an Associate Co. of A

- Company B1 and B2 are Subsidiaries of B and are the Step-Down Subsidiaries of Company A

Transactions With Subsidiary Companies/Associates/Sister Concerns

Transactions with sister concerns require close scrutiny since the modus operandi of most frauds has occurred through transactions with sister concerns. Despite the law requiring such transactions to be conducted at arm's length, they often exceed the limits through various colorable devices. This is facilitated by the common management and control over the company's transactions. Transactions with sister concerns are less transparent and more suspicious, indicating an intent to engage in fraudulent practices. This is one of the key areas where fraud occurs.

3.5.3 Foreign Companies

The term 'foreign company' is clearly defined under Section 2, subsection 42 of the Companies Act, 2013. A foreign company is any company or body corporate incorporated outside India that:

- Has a place of business in India, either physically or through electronic mode, directly or through an agent; and

- Conducts any business activity in India in any other manner.

In other words, a foreign company is a company registered outside India but having a place of business in India, which may also operate through electronic means. Even if the company's server is located outside India, it is still considered a foreign company as per the Companies Act 2013.

Foreign investment in domestic companies or the establishment of subsidiaries of foreign companies where funds from a third country are infused may involve the use of illegal money laundered into the company.

Sometimes, companies falsely portray themselves as subsidiaries of foreign companies, with foreign nationals as directors and foreign companies as shareholders, to fraudulently move money out of the country where they operate and avoid taxes, causing wrongful loss to the government of the country.

3.5.4 Internal Check

Internal check is a procedure whereby the work of one employee is automatically checked by another while performing routine duties. It is an essential function of the internal control system. For example,

Purchases of goods: Goods requisitions are received from different departments. The purchase department then invites quotations and places orders (orders are signed by the Purchase Manager). Goods received by the company or godown are entered into the store's ledger, and the gatekeeper has goods received the note. On receipt of invoices from the suppliers, the purchase department checks them against the goods received note and stores ledger, verifying quantity, rate, discount, etc. The accounts department makes the payment after verifying the invoice with the purchase order and goods received the note.

In the above example, it is evident that the work of one person is checked by another automatically while performing routine duties.

3.5.5 Internal Control

Internal control is a tool used by management and auditors to ensure proper operational efficiency and effectiveness in the company. It is a system that creates an audit trail for each transaction in the company. The management designs this system for monitoring wastage, protecting resources, detecting fraud, ensuring compliance with all company policies and procedures, and ensuring reliability in accounting data. An internal check is a part of the internal control system. Examples of internal control systems include

Segregation Of Duties (Division Of Labor): Duties of accounts writing and cashier are segregated so that one person does not have control over both books and cash, reducing the risk of wastage or fraud.

Authorizations At Various Levels For The Purchase Of Assets/Major Expenses: Companies may have a system of obtaining signatures from authorized personnel for transactions above a certain amount, reducing errors and the likelihood of fraud.

Reviews By Management: Management reviews transactions with significant amounts and conducts periodic performance reviews of employees to ensure alignment with company goals. Providing proper training and guidance, and maintaining standard operating procedures are also part of internal control.

Chapter 4

What Is Financial Statement Fraud? Modus Operandi Of Fraud And How To Start Investigation In Respect Of Items Of The Balance Sheet And Profit & Loss Account

4.1 What Is Financial Statement Fraud?

The Association of Certified Fraud Examiners (ACFE) defines accounting fraud as "deception or misrepresentation that an individual or entity makes, knowing that the misrepresentation could result in some unauthorized benefit to the individual, entity, or some other party." Thus, financial statement fraud occurs when a company misrepresents the figures on its financial statements to make them appear different from what it actually is.

Financial Statement Frauds Can Be Done Using The Following:

- Overstating/Understating Revenue.

- Understating/Overstating Expenses.

- Overvaluation/Undervaluation of Stock.

- Inflating the value of Assets (charging less depreciation or not writing off bad loans/investments).

- Writing off Assets.

- Writing Back liabilities.

- Fake related party transactions.

- Diversion of funds to subsidiaries and associated companies with the intention to misappropriate funds.

- Diversion of funds to shell companies created by the promoter company.

- Diversion of funds from company to personal with intent to create personal assets by misappropriating the funds of the company.

- Concealing or suppressing the income of the company with a view to making personal gains.

- Fraud through JVs (Journal Vouchers) by passing journal entries in the books of accounts.

4.2 Frauds By Journal Entries

One of the ways of committing financial fraud can be through passing Journal Entries. Journal Entries can be used to manipulate the accounts and alter the financial statements entirely, as no cash/bank accounts are involved in Journal Entries. With the help of journal entries, it becomes easy to manipulate accounting records. A journal entry has a debit effect and an equal-opposite credit effect. Let us see some examples of journal entries:

        Creditors A/c.................... Dr.
            To Debtors A/c

This entry is passed with the intention to write off both Debtors and Creditors at the same time, meaning that creditors and debtors are set off against each other. If debtors and creditors both belong to the same company, a set-off can be done. Otherwise, this entry may indicate ingenuine transactions and fraudulent activities within the company. It could be used to correct bogus purchases and sales that occurred in the past. Accordingly, these types of journal entries require in-depth investigation.

Bad Debts Written off:

        Bad Debts A/c.................... Dr.
            To Debtors A/c.

This entry is for writing off debtors. Bad Debts represent a loss and, thus, lower the profits of the company. At the same time, writing off bad debt may also indicate that the money, if received in cash from such a debtor, may have been siphoned off by not accounting for it in the books. Sometimes, debts from sister concerns are written off, and the same is siphoned off from the sister concern. Writing off bad debts may presuppose ingenuine/bogus turnover reflected in the past by the company. Accordingly, this aspect requires investigation.

Provision for Doubtful Debts:

        Profit & Loss A/c.................... Dr.
            To Provision for Doubtful Debts A/c

Provision for doubtful debts is created as a precautionary measure, assuming that a certain percentage of debtors to whom goods are sold on credit may not pay due to incapability or insolvency. It is generally taken as a percentage of Debtors. When this provision is no longer required, it is reversed. It can be used as a tool to increase or decrease the profits of the company. If a company creates a huge provision for doubtful debts on receivables from related parties, it is a red flag indicating ingenuine transactions with sister concerns.

Sundry Balances/Creditors written back:

    Creditors A/c.................... Dr.
        To Sundry Balances written back A/c

Sundry Balances written back can be the Creditor's balances that are no longer required to be paid and are written back. Creditors are generally for the purchase of goods or expenses, and the company may decide to write back the same if the portion of the balances is negligible and no longer payable. The amount is treated as income of the company. Thus, other incomes in the Profit & Loss account may contain Sundry Balances written back. However, if a huge amount of creditors' balances is written back, it is a red flag indicating ingenuine transactions of purchases.

Investments Written Off:

    Investments Written off A/c.................... Dr.
        To Investments A/c

Investments appear on the Asset side of the Balance Sheet. The value of investments needs to be reduced if investments are written off. Thus, the write-off portion becomes a loss for the company. One should check whether the company is writing off investments every year, the quantum of investments written off, etc. Investment with sister concerns, if written off, requires detailed investigation. One of the modus operandi to siphon off the funds of the company is through opening subsidiaries abroad and making investments in such foreign subsidiaries for the purpose of expanding the business. Later on, such investments are written off due to huge losses occurring in foreign subsidiaries.

4.3 Modus Operandi Of Financial Frauds Relating To Main Items Of Balance Sheet And How To Investigate

i. Fixed Assets

Modus Operandi	How To Investigate?
Fake Or Bogus Invoice (No Delivery Of Asset - Availing Bank Loan Fraudulently)	• Invoices for the purchase of fixed assets need to be checked along with supporting documents such as delivery challan, transport receipt, etc. Bank statements should be reviewed to verify payments made against the invoices. Vehicle details can be confirmed using applications like Car Info or www.vahan.parivahan.gov.in.
Overvalued Invoice (Intent To Indulge In Kickback Transactions)	• Request the installation report of the asset.
Undervalued Invoice (Intent To Evasion Of Customs Duty)	• Conduct a background check of vendors, including information about their establishment, factories, godowns, etc. The authenticity of vendors can be checked against GST defaulters' lists available on government websites, such as https://mahagst.gov.in/en/list/filers/143.

Undervalued Invoice (Intent To Evasion Of Customs Duty)	• Check if the assets purchased are relevant to the business of the company. • Verify the fixed asset register to determine its location and authenticity. • Check if the company has purchased fixed assets from its subsidiaries or associates and confirm if it was done at the market rate.
Purchase Of Fixed Assets Not Relevant To The Business Of The Company And Making Personal Use Of The Same	• For high-value transactions, ensure that a Board Resolution has been obtained. • Compare quotations received from different vendors, if applicable. • Investigate if there is any undervaluation of invoices and whether any other payments or advances were made to the vendor or their associates. • Study the nature of the expense and ascertain whether it is capital in nature or not. Analyze the nature, usefulness, and estimated life of the fixed asset.

ii. Intangible Assets

Modus Operandi	How to investigate?
Higher Valuation Of Goodwill (Overstated Assets; Overstated Forecasts For Future Profits)	• Please check the assumptions used for the valuation of goodwill. • Compare the future maintainable profits with the past profits. • Review the calculations of the fair market value of assets (if the net assets value method is considered). • Ensure there is a valuation report from a registered valuer.
Higher Valuation Of Patents And Trademarks (Total Expenditure On Research, Development As Well As Registration Expenses)	• Check whether operating expenditures, such as salaries, etc., are capitalized during the development period or not. • Sometimes, unnecessary expenditures not related to research and development are also capitalized (one needs to verify the genuineness of these expenditures). • Conduct a background check of researchers, such as scientists or experts appointed. • Verify whether the laboratories are installed or used to carry out R & D expenditures.

	• Ensure a copy of the Registration Certificate received under the Trademarks Act, 1999, is available.
Higher Valuation Of Copyrights	• Check the amount of research and development expenses made each year for the development of copyrights. • Verify whether operating expenditures, such as salaries, etc., are capitalized during the development period or not. • Sometimes, unnecessary expenditures not related to research are also capitalized (one needs to find out the genuineness of these expenditures). • Conduct a background check of researchers. • Ensure a copy of the Registration Certificate received is available.
Creation Of Tenancy Rights	• Check the premium paid for the acquisition of tenancy. • Review the tenancy agreement entered with the Landlord – details like tenant name, landlord's name, number of years of tenancy, monthly rent, etc. • Verify the bank statements of the tenant for a premium paid and monthly or yearly rent paid.

	• Obtain a copy of the letter of possession of the property.
	• Verify the physical existence of the property.
	• Determine the market value of the property by comparing it with the rates prevailing in the vicinity area.
	• Find out the unaccounted portion paid for acquiring tenancy rights.

iii. Long-Term Investments

Modus Operandi	How To Investigate?
Investment In: • Equity shares at a premium.	• Check the valuation of the company done by the Registered Valuer at the time shares are purchased at a premium.
• Equities of the Subsidiary and Associate Companies at higher/lower values.	• Review the assumptions on which the valuation of the company is based.
• Schemes of Demerger (overvalue/undervalue).	• Verify whether any key persons of investing companies hold substantial interest in the investee company.

• Schemes of Merger and Acquisition (overvalue/undervalue).	• Examine the bank transactions, i.e., payment made for the acquisition of shares and the source thereof.
• Long-term debenture fund (inadequate security).	• Verify the instrument of investment (Share certificate or debenture certificate in the name of the company).
• Employee floated companies (diversion of funds).	
• Foreign branch/Foreign subsidiaries (diversion and siphoning of funds).	

iv. Current Assets

Modus Operandi	How To Investigate?
Inventories (Stock) (Manipulation Of Quantity And Valuation Of Stock, Writing Off The Value Of Stock)	• Check the gross profit margin – whether there are any major differences compared to previous years, also compare it with the GP margin of similar companies in the same industry. • Compare the stock turnover ratio with the preceding years. Is the inventory in proportion to sales?

- Verify whether the valuation of stock is based on accounting policies and methods followed by the company. Also, check if the valuation of stock is consistently based on first-in-first-out (FIFO) or Last-in-first-out (LIFO) adopted by the company. Ensure that the valuation correlates with the value of purchases made by the company and that the rates applied to the number of stocks are in accordance with the method of accounting followed by the company.

- Check for any abnormal sales returns or purchase returns that happened during year-end or the start of the year.

- Confirm if a stock audit is conducted. If yes, obtain the valuation done by the stock auditor.

- Verify whether physical verification of stock is done and whether any qualified opinion is given by the auditor in case of material discrepancies in the physical verification of stock. Compare the closing inventory and its valuation with the Tax Audit report prepared under the Income Tax Act.

	- Compare the inventory quantity and value as per the stock register maintained by the company. Also, compare the valuation of stock with the value taken in the Profit & Loss Account.
Trade Receivables (Debtors) (Creation Of Debtors Using Subsidiaries, Associate Companies, And Shell Companies)	- Obtain the list of top debtors with their names, addresses, and balances as of a particular date. - Check whether the above list includes large amounts of debtors pertaining to related parties, such as subsidiary companies or associate companies. - Verify whether the debtors are backed by the actual sale of goods/services or by passing journal entries. - Compare the rates at which goods are sold to related parties with outside parties to determine whether the transactions are at arm's length with the related parties or not. If transfer pricing is applicable to the company, call for transfer pricing assessment orders passed by Income Tax authorities.

	- Examine the actual delivery of goods to related parties by verifying transport receipts and loading expenditure. This is one of the popular modus operandi to siphon out funds of the company into the hands of related parties. - Check whether debtors' write-offs or provisions for bad and doubtful debts are unusual or not. - If Bad Debts are written off during the year, take the names of debtors whose debts are written off and verify whether they include related parties or not. In case of large amounts written off, check whether the same is backed by a Board Resolution. - Check the discounts given to related party debtors and whether the same is as per market practice or not. - Check the debtor's collection period for unusual increases in the debtors' collection period, then verify whether the same pertains to related parties or not.

	• Examine the background of debtors to find out whether there are common directors between the company under investigation and the companies reflected as debtors.
Cash & Bank Balances (Bogus Fixed Deposit Receipts – Satyam Case)	• Check whether the cash balances are in proportion to sales or not. • Verify whether bank reconciliations are made for all banks. Obtain a copy of the bank reconciliation statement at the year-end. • Obtain bank confirmation certificates from the banks for bank balances and fixed deposits (FDs). • Cross-examine by obtaining certificates and statements of accounts from the bank to verify the genuineness of investments made with the bank, such as fixed deposits, etc.
Marketable Short-Term Investments (Fixed Deposit With Sister Concerns, Bank Receipts)	• Obtain the list of Marketable Short-Term investments company-wise. • Compare the investments with the previous year to determine additions or deletions. • Check whether any write-offs in listed/quoted investments have been made during any year.

	- In case of investments in unlisted/private limited companies, if there are any write-offs, check the documentation available for such write-offs (valuation report given by the registered valuer). - Check whether the value of investments is at cost or a revalued figure is reflected in the Balance sheet (with corresponding Revaluation Reserve under Reserves & Surplus).
Short-Term Loans & Advances (Loans To Sister Concerns, Advances To Fraudulent Non-Existing Person)	- Check the board resolution authorizing loans and advances given. - Verify whether any loan agreement is signed between the parties. - Check whether loans and advances given by the company are to any related parties, including any subsidiary, holding company, associate, related companies (with common directorship), relative of the director, or key managerial personnel. - Check whether interest is received on these loans or not. Verify if the rate of interest is as per prevailing market rates. - In case of non-receipt of interest/principal amount, check whether any action has been taken for the recovery of the same or not.

	- Examine whether any loans or advances have been given to foreign subsidiaries, foreign associates, or related parties in foreign countries. Check the terms of RBI permission obtained by the company. Also, verify whether any balances have been written off in such parties. Writing off loans given to foreign parties can be a red flag indicating siphoning off funds. - Request the annual financial statements of such foreign subsidiaries/associates to check for any diversion of funds given as loans to these foreign related parties. - Check the background of the parties to whom loans are given and verify if there are common directors/shareholders between the companies. - These items are of high importance in forensic investigation since most of the funds are diverted/siphoned out by this route, specifically, the diversion of funds outside India.

v. Shareholder's Funds

Modus Operandi	How To Investigate?
Equity & Preference Share Capital (Value Of The Shares Subscribed By Shareholders) (Money Laundering)	• Verify whether the shares are issued at par or at a premium. If the shares are issued at a premium, then obtain the valuation report given by a registered valuer. • If the shares are issued based on shareholder's agreements, request a copy of such agreements. • Check whether the shares are allotted to offshore companies. If yes, then obtain RBI permissions wherever applicable. • Request the bank statements of the company that invested in the company under investigation. • Conduct a background check of the company that invested money in the company under investigation, and also verify whether there are common directors between these two companies.

	• It is necessary to verify whether investing companies are directly or indirectly controlled by the company under investigation, as quite often, there are round-trippings of funds.
Reserves & Surplus: Past Retained Earnings (General Reserve) (Artificial Profits)	• Check whether reserves are artificially created by revaluing assets with the intent to grab a share premium from the investing company. Verify if the reserve is created as a revaluation reserve by inflating the value of assets or not. • To ascertain the genuineness of past profits, check whether they were created by artificial income or inflated turnover with the intent to grab a share premium from the investing company.

vi. Long-Term Borrowing (Bank/Financial Institution Frauds)

Modus Operandi	How To Investigate?
The Company May Have Borrowed Funds From Banks, Financial Institutions, And Related Parties. (Funds From Related Parties Or Offshore Companies May Be Routed Through Money Laundering)	• Call for the loan agreement, and verify the purpose of the loan, the security offered, and whether the funds obtained are utilized for the intended purpose. • Examine the invoices/agreements related to the purchases of assets made out of long-term borrowing. • Verify whether the assets purchased are being used for the purpose of the company's business. • Ensure that the assets purchased are installed at the company's business premises only. • Examine the relationship between the borrowing company and the lending company, especially if they have common directors, shareholders, etc. • Investigate whether any bank officials have created the company and introduced bank money into the investigating company. • Check whether the rate of interest paid to related parties is at market rates or not.

vii. Current Liabilities & Provisions

Modus Operandi	How To Investigate?
Trade Payables Fake Bills Fake Vendors (Increase The Purchases And Reduce The Net Profit)	• Call for a list of vendors and conduct a background check of the vendors to find out whether there are common directors/shareholders between the company under investigation and the vendor companies. • To verify the genuineness of purchases, check E-way bills, carriage inward, delivery challans, stores ledger, and lorry receipt. Also, cross-check purchases against GST returns. • Obtain balance confirmations from top creditors. • Request the names of creditors whose outstanding balances are for over 180 days. There is a high probability that there may be accommodation of bills, i.e., no goods received against the invoices raised. • Verify the items of purchase and correlate them with the business needs.

	• Check the status of all contingent liabilities. It is possible that any of these contingent liabilities have materialized and are payable but not reflected in the balance sheet, with the intention to display a rosy picture to attract investors.
Outstanding Expenses (Bogus Outstanding Expenses)	• Call for the list of outstanding expenditure along with copy of the bills raised by the vendors. • Call for the statements when these outstanding expenditures are paid in the subsequent year. • Call for the record of outstanding expenditure of more than 180 days. • Examine the nature of services rendered against the bills remained outstanding and whether the services were need of the business or not.
Bank Overdraft/ Cash Credit Facility (Bogus Valuation Of Stock, Debtors And Creditors):	• Call for sanction letters issued by the bank. • Examine the securities offered against Cash Credit facilities/Overdraft facilities. • Review the drawing power assessed by the bank on a month-to-month basis in case of cash credit facilities given.

- Request the stock statements, list of debtors and their valuation, and list of creditors and their value.

- Calculate the drawing power using the following formula: Drawing Power = 70% of (Value of Closing Stock + Value of Debtors − Value of Creditors for purchases and expenses).

- Call for the inspection report of the bank and the names of the officers who have visited for the physical verification of stock at the client's premises.

- Check from the list of debtors whether any of the parties are related parties or subsidiary companies.

- Verify whether the creditors are related parties or associate parties.

- If stock inspection is one of the conditions in the sanction letter, call for stock audit reports.

- Call for the Funds Flow statement from the company to examine whether cash credits have been utilized for the purpose of making payments to creditors or bills payable only.

	- Examine the Funds Flow statement to determine whether funds have been diverted to sister concerns or related parties from the cash credit facilities or not.
- Verify the correct valuation of stock and the stock register maintained by the company.
- This is the most important item in which maximum fraud takes place, and hence it is very much necessary to understand the concept of cash credit facilities.
Provisions (Artificial Provisions To Alter The Profits)	- Call for bills of the expenses provided for and examine their genuineness.
- Check if any provision is outstanding for more than a year (if so, then it might be an adjustment entry to show less profits).
- Request the records for the settlement of outstanding payments reflected in the Balance Sheet.
- Examine the names of the parties against which the provisions are made and verify whether they are related parties or not, having common directors.

4.4 Modus Operandi Of Financial Frauds Relating To Main Items Of Profit & Loss Account And How To Investigate

i. Sales/Turnover

Modus Operandi	How To Investigate?
Increasing Turnover (Fake Bills Or Sales To Subsidiaries, Associates, And Shell Companies With An Intent To Avail Bank Loan Or Attract Investors To Grab Share Premium)	• Call for the top 10 listed parties with whom the company made significant turnovers. • Examine sales transactions with related parties to check whether they are at arm's length or not. • Investigate unusual changes in the debtor's collection period. Look into debtors pending for more than 180 days. • Compare the sales with GST returns. • Examine the background of debtors to whom goods are sold on credit and verify whether there are common directors/shareholders or not. • Check the addresses of companies having a common address with the company under investigation. This will provide hints about artificial or fake turnover.

	• If there are cash sales, verify whether adequate internal controls with regard to cash sales are in place or not.
	• For export sales, examine the names of foreign debtors and find out if there are any common directors between the two companies.
	• Check the stock register to match the sales with the quantity of goods delivered.
	• Examine the delivery challan, E-way bill, and carriage outward expenditure to ascertain the genuineness of the transactions.

ii. Artificial Booking Of Other Income

Modus Operandi	How To Investigate?
To Sustain The Profitability Of The Company And To Show A Rosy Picture (Intent To Avail Bank Loan Or To Attract The Investors, Artificial Income Is Booked)	• Companies availing loans from banks/ financial institutions have to disclose adequate profits to renew or enhance their bank loan facilities. • If the business operations are not sufficient to generate enough profits, then, many times companies book artificial income in the form of the sale of scrap, job processing income, commission, brokerage income, etc.

- It is important to examine and request the names and addresses of the parties who have provided the income to the company under investigation.

- Conduct a background check of the companies that have provided income to the company under investigation and find out whether there are any common directors and shareholders between the two companies.

- In case of income received from a foreign company, examine the background check of the foreign company and also the remittances received through authorized banks.

- Examine the nature of services offered by the company and evaluate whether the company under investigation has the capacity to generate such income or not.

- Check the correlation between the activities of the company and the services offered by the company.

iii. Purchases

Modus Operandi	How To Investigate?
Introducing Fake Purchase Bills To Lower The Profits Of The Company (Intention To Diversify The Profits Of The Company To The Personal)	• Obtain the list of top 10 creditors. • Examine whether there are common directors and shareholders between the company under investigation and the creditors. • Obtain the list of creditors outstanding for more than 180 days and examine whether they are related parties or not. • Check purchases with GST returns. • Obtain balance confirmations from creditors. • Review material consumption reports. • To ascertain the genuineness of the purchases, examine the purchases with delivery challan, E-way bill, transport expenditure, and loading, and unloading expenditure. • Examine the purchases made from subsidiary and associate companies and verify the rates with the market rate of the same items. • Verify whether stocks are recorded in the stock register or not by examining stock records.

iv. Showing Artificial Profit On Sale Of Assets

Modus Operandi	How To Investigate?
Showing Artificial Profit On The Sale Of Assets	• Obtain a copy of the sale bill of the asset sold along with the name and address of the parties to whom it is sold. • Examine whether the parties are subsidiaries, associates, or related parties. • Check the depreciable value of the asset sold. • Find the reasons for discarding the asset. Determine whether the circumstances require the acquisition of a new machine. • Identify the method of selling the asset, such as auction sale, sale through a broker, or private agency.

v. Showing Artificial Profit On Sale Of Investments

Modus Operandi	How To Investigate?
Showing Artificial Profit On Sale Of Investments	• Obtain a copy of the sale bill of the asset sold along with the name and address of the parties to whom it is sold. • Examine whether the parties are subsidiaries, associates, or related parties.

	- Examine the book value and market value of the investment sold.
- If the investments are sold much below the market value, then examine whether there are common directors between the company under investigation and the company in which the investments were made.
- Find out the cost of this asset and from whom it was purchased. Determine if it is an investment in a listed or unlisted company.
- Identify the party to whom this investment is sold. Check whether there was any valuation of such investment in the case of unlisted company investment.

vi. Sundry Balances Written Back Through Bogus Creditors

Modus Operandi	How To Investigate?
Debts Payable To Related Parties Are Written Back (Higher Income)	- Call for a list of creditors whose balances are written back.
- Examine whether the creditors are subsidiaries or related companies.
- Review the original transactions of purchases and examine the genuineness of purchases through bills, challans, etc.

	• Investigate the reasons why such balances are not to be paid.

vii. Interest Income Through Loans To Subsidiaries And Associate Companies

Modus Operandi	How To Investigate?
Interest Income (Through Loans To Subsidiaries And Associate Companies)	• Check the amount of interest corresponding to the amount of loans. Verify whether interest is received/receivable on all loans or not. • Determine if the same rate of interest is provided on all loans or not, and scrutinize any unusually high or low-interest payments. • Examine whether the borrowings made from sister concerns are applied for the purpose of business or not.

viii. Rent Income Through Leasing To Related Parties

Modus Operandi	How To Investigate?
Rent Income Through Leasing To Related Parties	• Call for the documents like registered leave and license agreement and verify the prevailing rate of rent in the vicinity area.

	• Examine the deposits received on leasing the premises.
	• Check the terms and conditions of the leave and license agreement and verify whether they are in line with market practice or not.
	• Verify whether the subject matter of the property is recorded in the books of the company under investigation.
	• Request actual consumption of electricity bills of the tenant to ascertain whether premises are actually let or if it is just book entries.

ix. Administrative Expenses (Ghost Employees)

Modus Operandi	How To Investigate?
Ghost Employee's **Staff Welfare, Commission, Reimbursements**	• Check the payroll register to ensure that it is signed by the employees for the receipt of income monthly. • For employees using a biometric system for attendance, note that their biometrics won't be available. • Examine the salary registers for missing PAN, contact numbers, and residential addresses.

	• Call for KYC of all employees to ascertain whether any ghost employees are being paid.
	• Check EPF and ESIC records to ensure that all employees are covered.
	• Verify whether all employees have submitted savings details for tax return purposes, as some ghost employees might not have done so.
	• Review whether the salaries and other employee benefit expenses are proportionate to sales or industry standards.
	• Check the reimbursements made to employees, as very high or no reimbursements at all may indicate red flags.

x. Selling & Distribution Expenses

Modus Operandi	How To Investigate?
Fake Bills Of Advertising, Marketing Research, Hoardings, Etc.	• Obtain the list of vendors engaged in marketing the company's products/services. • Check whether the vendor companies are subsidiaries, associates, or have common directors.

- Apply the ratio of selling and distribution expenditure to turnover of the company for the last 3-5 years to ascertain any abnormalities under this head of expenditure.

- Request the list of commissions paid to persons or companies and ascertain whether they are related to directors or companies having common directorship.

- Obtain the percentage of commission paid to agents and verify whether it is in line with prevailing market practices.

- Review the letters or contracts entered with sales commission agents to ascertain whether they are responsible for collections against turnover or not.

- Collect information about experienced persons engaged in marketing research and request the documents prepared by them in connection with research-related activities.

- Check whether hoardings are displayed through space occupied by local authorities or advertising agencies that own the hoarding space.

xi. Finance Cost Through Subsidiaries And Associates

Modus Operandi	How To Investigate?
Higher Rate Of Interest To Subsidiary And Associate Companies	• Call for the list of lenders who financed the company under investigation. Check whether they have a valid NBFC license to advance money or not (except for intercorporate deposits). • Request the rate of interest paid against the finance obtained to ascertain whether it is in line with prevailing market practices or not. • Check the amount of interest corresponding to the amount of loans. Verify whether interest is provided on all loans or not. • Determine whether the interest is actually paid or if only provisions are made against the money borrowed.

xii. Bad Debts Written Off Through Bogus Debtors

Modus Operandi	How To Investigate?
Fictitious Sales-Related Party Transactions (Writing Off Bad Debts Against The Collection From Subsidiaries And Associate Companies)	• Call for the list of parties against which debts are written off as bad. • Check whether the aforementioned list includes subsidiaries, associates, or related parties or not. • Verify whether bad debts written off pertain to foreign subsidiaries/foreign companies or not. • Request the original sales invoices along with delivery challan proof against which outstanding payments are written off as bad debt. • Inquire whether adequate legal action has been taken against such debtors before writing them off as bad debt. • Check whether the debtor's companies and the company under investigation have common directors or not. • Verify whether the debtors against which bad debts are written off continue their business activities in the market or not.

	• Examine the bad debts to sales ratio for the three preceding years to find any unusual increase or decrease in bad debts.
	• This item is very important from a forensic investigation point of view since many frauds occur through making turnovers to sister concerns and then writing off the recovery from them.

xiii. Over/Understated Loss On Sale Of Assets

Modus Operandi	How To Investigate?
Over/Understated Loss On Sale Of Assets Resulting In Wrongful Loss To The Company	• Call for the list of assets sold during the year along with the name and address of the parties to whom the assets are sold. • Check whether the assets are sold privately, through bidding, or through an auction sale. • Verify whether the assets are sold to subsidiaries, associates, or related parties. • Request the useful life of the asset sold and check whether it was sold on completion of the useful life.

xiv. Over/Understated Loss On Sale Of Unquoted Investments

Modus Operandi	How To Investigate?
Over/Understated Loss On Sale Of Unquoted Investments Resulting Into Wrongful Loss To The Company	• Call for the list of investments sold during the year along with the name and address of the parties to whom the investments are sold. • Check whether the investments are sold privately, through bidding, or through an auction sale. • Verify whether the investments are sold to subsidiaries, associates, or related parties. • Find out if there was any valuation of such an investment. Call for the valuation report and compare the sale price with the valuation report. • Check whether the investments made in foreign subsidiaries are sold and whether RBI permission is obtained or not.

xv. Investments Written Off In Unlisted Subsidiaries And Associate Company

Modus Operandi	How To Investigate?
Making Investments In Unlisted Subsidiaries And Subsequently Writing Them Off, Causing Wrongful Loss To The Company By Diversion Of Funds	• Call for the names and addresses of the subsidiaries, including foreign subsidiaries, in which investments were made. Also, request permission obtained from RBI at the time of making foreign investments. • Check whether adequate securities were obtained while making investments in the related companies. • Verify whether the securities obtained were genuine and sufficient at the time of making investments. • Request the valuation report obtained at the time of making investments in subsidiary companies. • Examine the losses incurred in subsidiary companies and the reasons thereof. • Call for the board resolution before writing off investments in subsidiaries. • Obtain the last five years' Balance sheets of the subsidiaries to ascertain whether the losses declared by the subsidiary are genuine or not.

4.5 Information Available On The MCA Website

Investigating officer has to obtain basic information about the company and its directors by downloading from the MCA website: www.mca.gov.in. The important information available on the MCA website can be tabulated as under

Purpose Of Form	Form No. (Companies Act, 2013)	Remarks
Notice of the situation or change of situation of the registered office and verification/change of the registered office within the same locality.	INC-22	For a change in the registered office within the same locality.
Application to the Regional Director for approval to shift the Registered Office from one State to another State or from the jurisdiction of one Registrar to another Registrar within the same State.	INC-23	For a change in registered office from one state to another or from one Registrar to another.

Application for the approval of the Central Government for a change of name.	INC-24	Application for change in the name of the company.
Conversion of a public company into a private company or a private company into a public company.	INC-27	Conversion of a public company to private or private to public.
Return of allotment.	PAS-3	Whenever a company having a share capital makes any allotment of securities, it shall file with the Registrar a return of allotment.
Private placement offer letter.	PAS-4	The copy of the record of offers and the private placement offer letter in Form PAS-4 should be filed with the ROC.
Application for the registration of creation or modification of charge (other than those related to debentures).	CHG-1	Registration of creation/ modification of charge.

Particulars for satisfaction of charge thereof.	**CHG-4**	Paying off/satisfaction of charge.
Application for registration of creation or modification of charge for debentures or rectification of particulars filed in respect of creation or modification of charge for debentures.	**CHG-9**	Creation, modification of charge for debentures.
Return for the declaration of beneficial interest in any shares.	**MGT-6**	Persons whose name is written in the register of shareholders but do not hold any beneficial interest in shares.
Annual Return.	**MGT-7**	Form MGT-7 is the form for filing annual returns by a company. The due date for filing MGT-7 is 60 days from the date of the Annual General Meeting.

Filing of resolutions and agreements to the Registrar under Section 117.	MGT-14	Filing certain resolutions with the Registrar of Companies.
Return of changes in the shareholding position of promoters and top 10 shareholders (Listed Companies).	MGT-10	Changes in the shareholding position of the top 10 shareholders of a listed company.
Appointment of auditor	ADT-1	To intimate the Registrar of Companies regarding the appointment of an auditor.
Application to the CG for removal of auditor before expiry of the term.	ADT-2	Application for removal of auditor before expiry of his term.
Resignation of an auditor (Intimation to Registrar by the auditor).	ADT-3	Resignation intimation to the registrar by the auditor.
Form to report any suspected fraud by Auditor to Central Government.	ADT-4	Reporting any suspected fraud by the auditor to Central Government.

Application for allotment of Director Identification Number.	**DIR-3**	Application for allotment of DIN.
Notice of the resignation of a director to the Registrar.	**DIR-11**	Resignation of Director.
Particulars of appointment of Directors and the key managerial personnel and the changes amongst them.	**DIR-12**	Appointment of Directors or KMP and any changes in Director or KMP.
Information to be filed by a foreign company.	**FC-1**	Details of the places of business other than the principal place of business in India. Details of the places of business established at any earlier occasion(s) Particulars of the authorized representatives.

Return of alteration in the documents filed for registration by a foreign company.	FC-2	Alteration in any documents filed for registration by a foreign company.
List of all principal places of business in India established by a foreign company.	FC-3	Every foreign company is required to prepare and file financial statements within a period of six months of the close of the financial year.
Intimation - Annual Return of a Foreign company.	FC-4	Annual Return of a Foreign Company.
Filing statement containing salient features of the financial statement of subsidiaries/ associate/joint venture companies.	AOC-1	AOC-1 shall require to be prepared by the Company where a company has one or more subsidiaries.
Filing XBRL documents in respect of Financial Statements & other documents.	AOC-4 XBRL	Information and Particulars in respect of Balance sheet and Profit & Loss; Reporting of CSR; Disclosure about Related Party Transactions; Audit Report and others.

Form for filing consolidated financial statements and other documents with the Registrar.	**AOC-4 (CFS)**	Form AOC 4 is used to file the financial statements for each financial year with the Registrar of Companies (ROC). In the case of consolidated financial statements, the company shall file the AOC 4 CFS.
Form for filing financial statements and other documents with the Registrar for NBFCs	**AOC-4 (NBFC)**	All NBFCs and their subsidiaries, holding, associate companies or joint ventures having a net worth of Rs.500 crore or more are required to fill the same information as under AOC-4 XBRL.

Chapter 5

Indicators Of Financial Statement Red Flags – Through Ratio Analysis And Computer-Assisted Software

5.1 Ratios

1. Increase In Sales But Non-Proportional Increase In The Cost Of Goods Sold

Ideally, when sales increase, the cost associated with these goods, like purchases/manufacturing, freight/carriage, etc., should also increase proportionately. If there is a disproportion between the two, it is a red flag. It might be possible that the company has adopted cost-reduction techniques.

2. Gross Profit Margin

Gross profit margin ratio is worked out as Gross profit divided by Sales and is shown as a percentage.

(Gross Profit/Net Sales) * 100

Generally, the gross profit ratio remains constant year after year as it takes into account the cost of goods, which remains proportional to sales. Thus, an unusual increase or decrease in the gross profit ratio is a red flag to be investigated.

3. Operating Ratio

The operating ratio is found to calculate all costs of operating as a percentage of Sales.

[(Cost of Goods Sold + Operating Expenses)/Net Sales] * 100

Generally, the operating ratio remains constant as a percentage of sales unless a very good cost-saving measure is adopted by the company during the year. Thus, an unusual increase or decrease in the operating ratio is a red flag to be investigated.

4. Net Profit Margin

Net Profit margin ratio is found to calculate Net profit as a percentage of sales.

(Net Profit/Net Sales) * 100

Net profit margin remains more or less constant year after year unless the company has adopted very good cost-saving measures during the year. An unusual increase/decrease in the net profit margin ratio is a red flag to be investigated.

5. Debtor's Collection Period

The debtor's collection period ratio indicates the number of days debtors remain outstanding.

(Average Debtors/Credit Sales) * 365

Average Debtors = (Opening Debtors + Closing Debtors)/2

In case of an increase or decrease in sales, the debtor's collection period remains generally constant. Changes in the collection strategy might change the ratio. The lower the collection period, the better for the company.

6. Stock Velocity Ratio

This ratio shows the number of days Inventory is held in stock. A lower number of days is considered better as the amount blocked in inventory is less.

(Average Inventory/Cost of Goods Sold) * 365

Average inventory = (Opening Stock + Closing Stock)/2

Cost of Goods sold = (Opening Stock + Purchases – Closing Stock)

Overvaluation or undervaluation of closing stock affects this ratio too. Thus, an unusual increase or decrease in this ratio indicates a red flag to be investigated.

7. Current Ratio

Current ratio of the company shows the short-term liquidity position of the company. The ratio is calculated as Current Assets/Current Liabilities.

A ratio of 2:1 is considered good, which means for payment of every one rupee of current liability, the company has Rs. 2 of current assets. But this standard ratio depends upon the nature of the business and type of industry. This ratio is also known as the working capital ratio. In the case of businesses where just in time, technology is adopted – inventory will be almost nil; in the case of cash counter businesses – debtors will be nil. Thus, in such cases, even a 1:1 current ratio is good. In case the company has concealed its current liabilities or shown current liabilities as long-term, this ratio will show a very good picture of the short-term liquidity. An unusual increase or decrease in the current ratio indicates a red flag to be investigated.

8. Quick Ratio

Quick ratio of the company shows the immediate liquidity position of the company. The ratio is calculated as:

Quick Assets/Quick Liabilities

Quick Assets = Current Assets – Stock – Prepaid Expenses

Quick Liabilities = Current Liabilities – Bank Overdraft

This ratio shows the company's ability to pay immediate cash for immediate liabilities. This ratio is also known as the liquid ratio. 1:1 is considered a good standard ratio for this. This means for every Re. 1 of quick liabilities, the company has Re. 1 of quick assets. An unusual increase in the ratio might also mean that fictitious sales bills are added and, thus, an increase in debtors. This means an unusual increase or decrease in this ratio requires investigation.

9. Debt-Equity Ratio

This ratio shows the risk position of the company.

Total Long-Term Debt/Equity

Equity = Share capital + Reserves

This ratio indicates the proportion of debt to equity. A ratio higher than one indicates the company depends more on outside funds than the owner's funds. An unusual increase or decrease in the ratio should be checked. If new loans are taken, issuance of shares or repayment of loans is found from cash flow, and it is okay. Otherwise, the increase or decrease needs to be investigated.

5.2 Computer-Assisted Techniques To Detect Red Flags

In modern times, various computer-assisted techniques are used in the normal course of auditing as well as for forensic investigation. A software called IDEA is popularly used for forensic investigation. IDEA is an advanced software compared to Microsoft Excel. It is more useful when there is a large volume of data, and specific information is required from the data. IDEA software helps us to analyze large data in a short period of time and evaluate the same in a manner we require for the purpose of investigation. The software imports various financial data from the soft copy of bank statements or accounting packages and synchronizes the same in a manner the information is required. It has facilities for putting certain keywords. With the help of keywords, we get specified financial information that we require for the purpose of investigation.

5.3 RBI Master Circular – Early Warning Signals

RBI Master Circular DBS.CO.CFMC.BC.No.1/23.04.001/2016-17 dated 1st July 2016 and revised on 3rd July 2017 state the following Early Warning Signals about wrongdoings in loan accounts that may turn fraudulent:

1. a) Default in undisputed payment to the statutory bodies as declared in the Annual report.

    a. Bouncing of high-value cheques.

    b. Frequent changes in the scope of the project to be undertaken by the borrower.

2. Foreign bills remaining outstanding with the bank for a long time and a tendency for bills to remain overdue.

3. Delay observed in the payment of outstanding dues.

4. Frequent invocation of BGs and devolvement of LCs.

5. Underinsured or overinsured inventory.

6. Invoices devoid of TAN and other details.

7. Dispute on the title of collateral securities.

8. Funds coming from other banks to liquidate the outstanding loan amount unless in the normal course.

9. In merchanting trade, the import leg is not revealed to the bank.

10. Requests received from the borrower to postpone the inspection of the godown for flimsy reasons.

11. Funding of interest by sanctioning additional facilities. Exclusive collateral charged to a number of lenders without NOC of existing charge holders.

12. Concealment of certain vital documents like master agreement and insurance coverage.

13. Floating front/associate companies by investing borrowed money.

14. Critical issues highlighted in the stock audit report. Liabilities appearing in the ROC search report are not reported by the borrower in its annual report.

15. Frequent requests for general-purpose loans. Frequent ad hoc sanctions.

16. Not routing sales proceeds through consortium I member banks/lenders to the company.

17. LCs issued for local trade I-related party transactions without underlying trade transactions.

18. High-value RTGS payment to unrelated parties.

19. Heavy cash withdrawal in loan accounts.

20. Non-production of original bills for verification upon request.

21. Significant movements in inventory, disproportionately differing vis-à-vis change in turnover.

22. Significant movements in receivables, disproportionately differing vis-à-vis change in turnover and/or increase in the aging of the receivables.

23. Disproportionate change in other current assets.

24. Significant increase in working capital borrowing as a percentage of turnover. Increase in Fixed Assets without a corresponding increase in long-term sources (when the project is implemented).

25. Increase in borrowings, despite huge cash and cash equivalents in the borrower's balance sheet.

26. Frequent change in the accounting period and/or accounting policies. Costing of the project is in wide variance with the standard cost of installation of the project.

27. Claims not acknowledged as debt high. Substantial increase in unbilled revenue year after year.

28. A large number of transactions with interconnected companies and large outstanding from such companies.

29. Substantially related party transactions. Material discrepancies in the annual report.

30. Significant inconsistencies within the annual report (between various sections).

31. Poor disclosure of materially adverse information and no qualification by the statutory auditors.

32. Raid by Income tax/sales tax/central excise duty officials.

33. Significant reduction in the stake of the promoter/director or an increase in the encumbered shares of the promoter/director.

34. Resignation of key personnel and frequent changes in management.

Chapter 6

Banking Fraud Investigation

6.1 Steps For Verification From Loan Application To Declaring It As A Fraud

6.2 Types Of Different Establishments And Liabilities Of Person

a. <u>Proprietorship:</u> It is a form of establishment in which a single person is the owner of the business. A bank account can be opened based on the KYC documents of the owner. The Permanent Account Number (PAN) of the proprietor and the business are the same. No other document is needed to start a proprietorship business. GSTIN can also be obtained for the proprietorship concern. A proprietorship concern is also called a sole proprietorship, and the owner is responsible for all the acts/liabilities of the business. The owner and the business are treated as one and the same entity.

b. <u>Partnership Firm:</u> A partnership form of business has a minimum of 2 partners and a maximum of 50. It is governed by the Partnership Act of 1932. A Deed of Partnership is required to be made before starting a partnership firm. A partnership has to apply for its own Permanent Account Number. A separate GSTIN, TAN, and other statutory identifications can be obtained under the name of the firm. Though the partnership is a separate legal entity, different from its partners, the liability of partners is unlimited, and there is a joint liability for all partners.

c. <u>Hindu Undivided Family:</u> This is popularly known as HUF. HUF is a Hindu family business. Hindus, Jains, Sikhs, and Buddhists can form HUF. A single person cannot form HUF. At the time of marriage, HUF is automatically created. Generally, a HUF deed is done where the common ancestral property is transferred to HUF. HUF is a separate legal entity from the members. The head of HUF is known as Karta, who is responsible for the management of the business. The liability of members of HUF is limited, but the liability of Karta is unlimited.

d. <u>Association of Persons (AOP)/Body of Individuals (BOI)</u>: When two or more persons come together for a common objective, they can form an AOP or BOI. In the case of AOP, any person, i.e., individuals, firms, companies, etc., can come together, whereas, in the case of BOI, only individuals are involved. A deed can be signed by members of AOP/BOI for its formation. In case of any fraud against AOP/BOI, the governing body, which manages the affairs of AOP/BOI, is liable.

e. <u>Company:</u> A company is a separate legal entity different from its members and is governed by the Companies Act 2013. Companies can be created following the procedure under the Companies Act 2013. There can be a Private Limited Company or a Public Limited Company.

f. <u>Private limited companies have a minimum of 2 members and a maximum of 200 members:</u> In the case of Public limited companies, a minimum of 7 members is required. Public limited companies can be a Listed company (i.e., listed on any Stock Exchange), or it can be an unlisted public company. Ownership in a company is based on the share certificate held by the shareholders. The share certificate can be in physical form or demat form. Share certificates can be transferred to another entity. In a private limited company, share certificates cannot be transferred at the whims of the holder. The articles of association of the company lay out the rules and regulations to transfer such shares. Transferring shares without following the rules laid down in the articles of association is void.

g. <u>The company has its own PAN:</u> The liability of members/shareholders is limited to the unpaid amount of shares held by them. Since the management of the company is the responsibility of elected representatives of shareholders called Directors, the liability arising due to the conduct of the business of the company rests with directors, which is discussed under the section "Liabilities of Directors" in this book.

h. <u>One-Person Company:</u> It is a new form of establishment registered under the Companies Act 2013. Compliance requirements are lesser than that of a private company. This is a single-member company having a single director (the director and member can be the same person). This form of establishment enjoys the benefits of both a company and a sole proprietorship. Thus, the liability in case of fraud is on the director, and the liability of the shareholder remains limited.

i. <u>Limited Liability Partnership</u>: It is an establishment that combines the merits of both a partnership firm and a company. Thus, the management is done like a partnership firm, but the liability of the partners is limited like a company. Thus, it is a separate legal entity, different from its partners. In case of any fraud, the LLP is responsible, and the partners' liability is unlimited.

j. <u>Government Company:</u> These are the companies under which 51% or more share capital is held by either the State Government, Central Government, or both. It is a separate legal entity. In case of any fraud against the company, the shareholders' liabilities are limited to the unpaid amount of shares held by them. Since it is managed by elected representatives of shareholders called directors, their liabilities are the same as liabilities of directors for any other company under the Companies Act, which is discussed under the section "Liabilities of Directors."

k. <u>Section 8 Company</u>: It is a company established to promote art, science, sports, research, etc., and the profits of such a company are not distributed to the members but are applied to the cause for which the company is created. The procedure for the creation of this type of establishment is the same as the procedure for the creation of a company. It is just like a limited liability company, where the liability of members is limited to the unpaid amount of shares held by them. Since it is managed by elected representatives of shareholders called directors, their liabilities are the same as liabilities of directors for any other company under the Companies Act, which is discussed under the section "Liabilities of Directors."

6.3 Types Of Bank Loans

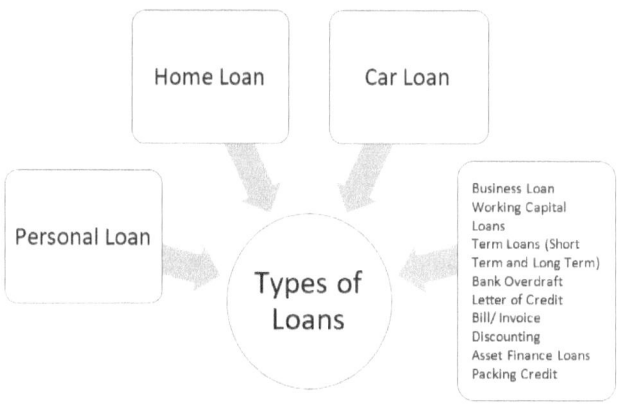

6.4 Non-Performing Assets (NPA)

(RBI Circular DOR.STR.REC.5/21.04.048/2022-23 dated 1st April 2022)

A non-performing asset is a loan or an advance where:

(i) Interest and/or installment of principal remain overdue for a period of more than 90 days in respect of a Term Loan.

(ii) The account remains 'out of order' in respect of an Overdraft/ Cash Credit (OD/CC) and all other loan products being offered as an overdraft facility, including those not meant for business purposes and/or which entail interest repayments as the only credits.

(iii) The bill remains overdue for a period of more than 90 days in the case of bills purchased and discounted.

(iv) Any amount to be received remains overdue for a period of more than 90 days in respect of other accounts.

6.5 Wilful Default

(Rbi Circular Br.No.Cid.Bc.57/20.16.003/2014-15 Dated 1st July 2014 And Revised On 7th July 2015)

(RBI Circular BR.No.CID.BC.57/20.16.003/2014-15 dated 1st July 2014, and revised on 7th July 2015)

A "wilful default" would be deemed to have occurred if any of the following events are noted:-

(a) The unit has defaulted in meeting its payment/repayment obligations to the lender even when it has the capacity to honor the said obligations.

(b) The unit has defaulted in meeting its payment/repayment obligations to the lender and has not utilized the finance from the lender for the specific purposes for which finance was availed but has diverted the funds for other purposes.

(c) The unit has defaulted in meeting its payment/repayment obligations to the lender and has siphoned off the funds so that the funds have not been utilized for the specific purpose for which finance was availed of, nor are the funds available with the unit in the form of other assets.

(d) The unit has defaulted in meeting its payment/repayment obligations to the lender and has also disposed of or removed the movable fixed assets or immovable property given by him or it for the purpose of securing a term loan without the knowledge of the bank/lender.

THEREFORE, Wilful default broadly covers the following:

(a) Deliberate non-payment of the dues despite adequate cash flow and good net worth;

(b) Siphoning off of funds to the detriment of the defaulting unit;

(c) Assets financed either not been purchased or been sold and proceeds have been mis-utilized;

(d) Misrepresentation/falsification of records;

(e) Disposal/removal of securities without the bank's knowledge;

(f) Fraudulent transactions by the borrower.

Pursuant to the instructions of the Central Vigilance Commission for collection of information on wilful defaults of Rs. 25 lakhs and above by RBI and dissemination to the reporting banks and FIs, a scheme was framed by RBI with effect from 1st April 1999 under which the banks and notified All India Financial Institutions were required to submit to RBI the details of the wilful defaulters.

Banks/FIs were advised that they should examine all cases of wilful defaults of Rs 1.00 crore and above for filing of suits and also consider criminal action wherever instances of cheating/fraud by the defaulting borrowers were detected. In the case of consortium/multiple lending, banks and FIs were advised that they report wilful defaults to other participating/financing banks also.

In order to prevent access to the capital markets by the wilful defaulters, a copy of the list of wilful defaulters (non-suit filed accounts) and a list of wilful defaulters (suit filed accounts) are forwarded to SEBI by RBI and Credit Information Bureau (India) Ltd. (CIBIL) respectively.

Criminal Action by Banks/FIs: It is essential to recognize that there is scope, even under the existing legislation, to initiate criminal action against wilful defaulters depending upon the facts and circumstances of the case under the provisions of Sections 403 and 415 of the Indian Penal Code (IPC) 1860. Banks/FIs are, therefore, advised to seriously and promptly consider initiating criminal action against wilful defaulters or wrong certification by borrowers, wherever considered necessary, based on the facts and circumstances of each case under the above provisions of the IPC

6.6 Sarfaesi Act

Securitization and Reconstruction of Financial Assets and Enforcement of Security Interest Act, 2002, is popularly called as SARFAESI Act, 2002. SARFAESI Act was enacted to safeguard the interest of Banks and financial institutions. The act provided that banks and financial institutions could seize the property of the borrower, in the case of secured loans, without going for court proceedings (Except for agricultural land). In the case of unsecured loans, banks would have to go to civil courts against the defaulters.

The act provides for the establishment of Asset Reconstruction Companies, which acquire bad loans from banks or financial institutions and recover the debts. The Act provides the time of 1-2 years for investigations and disposal of the case.

Due to the delayed and non-efficiency of the SARFAESI Act, the Insolvency and Bankruptcy Code was drafted and put into effect. Once a case is admitted under IBC, the SARFAESI Act has no jurisdiction over the said case.

6.7 Insolvency and Bankruptcy Code

The Insolvency and Bankruptcy Code were enacted in 2016. It came into force on 28th May 2016. The intention of proposing this act was the mounting pressure of Non-Performing Assets (NPAs) and non-payment of dues by the entity to the bank, its operational creditor,

NBFC, etc. The apex body under this Act is the IBBI (Insolvency and Bankruptcy Board of India).

This law sets out three classes of persons who can initiate the Corporate Insolvency Resolution Process:

- Operational Creditor - as per Section 8 of the act
- Financial Creditor – as per Section 7 of the act
- Corporate Applicant (employees or shareholders) under Corporate Debtor – as per section 10 of the act

The entity against whom the IBC proceedings are initiated is called the corporate debtor. In the case of Companies and LLPs, the Insolvency petition can be submitted by any of the above classes of persons with NCLT (National Company Law Tribunal), whereas, in the case of individuals and partnerships, it can be submitted to the Debt Recovery Tribunal.

Once an insolvency petition is admitted, a moratorium is introduced, which remains in force till the end of CIRP. During the moratorium period, no judicial proceedings, including criminal proceedings except proceedings against the PMLA Act, against the company can be held. This means that the assets of the corporate debtor are saved from further depletion. A resolution professional is appointed who submits a resolution plan, and if taken up, the company can be revived, but if the resolution plan fails, then the company is liquidated. The Act has set a timeline of 180 days for the Corporate Insolvency Resolution Process (CIRP), which can be extended further to 90 days. The time limit of 180 days begins from when the IBC professional and the committee of creditors approve the CIRP plan.

Chapter 7
Criminal Prosecution

After completion of the investigation, the Investigating Officer, with the approval of the Station House Officer (SHO), has to file the final report known as the Charge Sheet, along with the following endorsement:

1. If the charge-sheeted accused person/s is a public servant, the IO has to make an endorsement that after receiving the sanction order from the competent authority, it will be filed in the court in due course.

2. This case will be conducted on behalf of the state by the public prosecutor/special prosecutor notified by the Government of Maharashtra/Central Government.

3. Further investigation will be in progress under section 173(8) of CrPC.

4. Cognizance of these offenses may be taken, and the trial may proceed as per the law.

After filing the Chargesheet, the court has to take cognizance of section 190 of CrPC. The Prosecution has to submit copies of all relied-upon statements of prosecution witnesses and copies of documents relied upon for all accused persons, along with one copy for the conducting Public Prosecutor. The Muddemal articles and crime properties are deposited in the court Malkhana.

The prosecution has to open the case with their arguments to frame the charges against each accused person by the court. If the accused persons have the right to file a discharge application on the grounds of "Charges are groundless," the court can decide on the application's merits after hearing both parties.

The prosecution should start an argument for framing charges, and after perusing the entire chargesheet, charges will be framed, and the Hon'ble court may direct the prosecution to take necessary steps to lead the evidence. The prosecution has to give notice under section 294 of CrPC for the admission or denial of relied-upon documents.

Further, the Prosecution has to start the case by presenting witnesses in the court, and the trial proceeds. The prosecution then files for the closing of evidence.

Based on the prosecution's evidence, the court will record the statements of the accused persons under section 313 of CrPC. The court can also examine the accused as a witness. The accused have the option to lead defense witnesses/evidence, if any.

Then, the Prosecution begins with final arguments to prove/support the Prosecution's evidence. After the Prosecution's arguments, the defense arguments take place. The Prosecution can give additional arguments, if any, along with relevant case laws of the Hon'ble High Court and Hon'ble Supreme Court. The Prosecution may also submit a Memorandum of Arguments. Thereafter, the case is adjourned for a verdict.

On the day of judgment, the Prosecution has to argue for the maximum punishment of imprisonment as per the law. The court has the discretion to give a lesser sentence as prescribed under the law, providing detailed reasons and grounds.

If the sentence is more than three years, the convicted person must be taken into judicial custody by the judiciary. If the sentence is less than three years, then the convicted accused person can be released on bail.

After the period of limitation for filing a criminal appeal before the Appellate court, the Prosecution has to move an application before the court for the issuance of a non-bailable warrant/arrest warrant against the convicted persons. If the accused is not traceable, the prosecution has to file an application for the proclamation order against the offender.

If the offender/convicted person does not surrender before the court during the period of proclamation, the Prosecution has to file an application for the attachment of the properties of the convicted person.

Chapter 8

Case Studies

Case Study 1: Grab And Go

Window-dressing of Financial Statements for False Valuation of the Company for grabbing fictitious premium from investors

Profit & Loss Account items involved: Sales A/c & Expenditure A/c

Balance Sheet items involved: Opening of Shell Companies and Fund Transfer, Debtors, Advances are given, Fictitious Creditors

Company Involved: Luckin Coffee Inc.

Period of Fraud: April 2019 to January 2020 (10 months)

Introduction

The Luckin Coffee (Luckin) coffeehouse chain was founded in 2017 on an innovative "grab and go" business model that allows its customers to order coffee and other convenience products via an app. Luckin Coffee got listed on Nasdaq (US Stock Market) in May 2019. By the end of 2019, Luckin was operating more than 4,500 stores throughout

China, with plans to expand in the Middle East and India. Luckin raised more than $864 million from debt and equity investors between April 2019 and January 2020.

Fraud

From April 2019 through January 2020, Luckin intentionally fabricated more than $300 million in retail sales by using related parties to create false sales transactions through three separate purchasing schemes (i.e., sale of fabricated coupons to individuals, corporate customers, and shell companies) along with inflating the company's expenses by more than $190 million so that they were consistent with the overstated revenue. Luckin returned the funds to the shell companies through bank transfers and fabricated business-related expenditures.

Consequences

On April 2, 2020, Luckin announced that it had suspended its CEO and several other staff members following suspicions that they had fabricated some transactions between Q3 and Q4 2019. Luckin, whose American Depositary Shares traded on Nasdaq until July 13, 2020, has agreed to pay a $180 million penalty to resolve the charges.

Relevant Sections Of The Indian Penal Code (Ipc) Involved

Section 477A (Falsification of Books of Accounts), 420 (Cheating), 471 (Creation of documents for the purpose of cheating by manipulating books of accounts).

References

www.asia.nikkei.com

www.sevenpillarsinstitute.org

www.reuters.com

Case Study 2: Drive Down Costs and Defer Expenses

Modus Operandi

Window-dressing of Financial Statements by the overvaluation of stock, inflated turnover

Profit & Loss Account Items involved: Sales A/c & Overvaluation of Closing Stock

Balance Sheet items involved: Opening of Shell Companies, Debtors, Overvaluation of Closing Stock

Company Involved: Sarkar Electronics (Names changed)

Introduction

Sarkar Electronics was incorporated in Delhi in 1960 as a supplier of electric bulbs for the automotive industry. A huge order from an automotive supplier in Canada made way for its first manufacturing plant in India. In 1999, the company opened its second manufacturing plant in Toronto, Canada, which later became the Canada Headquarters.

Siddharth Malhotra, an ambitious man, had been working in this company for over 30 years and was appointed as the new CEO of the Canada subsidiary, assuring his future with the company headquarters in India.

Fraud

a. The Canadian subsidiary was performing exceptionally well enough to wipe out the entire accumulated deficit that the company had. Unfortunately, Sarkar Electronics' surge in the market came to a halt. The company issued strict directives to all foreign subsidiaries to cut expenses and expand sales to meet the revised and aggressive financial goals.

b. To meet the impossible standards set by the India Headquarters, Malhotra pushed his team to drive down costs and defer expenses but still could not meet the expectations. Malhotra used internal bills of lading, which were generally ignored by auditors, signifying inter-company transfers to falsify sales as though they were made to third parties. Malhotra further concealed the fraudulent transactions by setting up fictitious companies to confirm sales made at year-end. These were made to entities no longer doing business with Sarkar Electronics and in quantities that would not raise questions. He also made sure all the addresses were under the PO boxes under his control.

c. The Canada subsidiary was to provide its financial statements before Sarkar Electronics posted its financial results. During the audit of the Canada subsidiary, Malhotra purposely held back inventory schedules till the very end of the audit, which in previous years were performed in the initial stages of the audit. On further inquiry with the CFO and the controller, they assured me that the reconciliation between book stock and physical inventory would be resolved within a week. Based on his instinct, the auditor started to verify the inventory binders. He found that the numbering of inter-company inventory transfers was out of sequence with the remaining bills of lading, ultimately finding that the inventory was misstated by several million dollars, which would wipe out the entire net income. Apparently, he received a private communication from India demanding a stronger financial performance in Canada, which would lead to a faster promotion.

Consequences

The CEO was "transferred" to a small subsidiary in India, thereby ruining his career. He was fortunate enough that he could not be prosecuted for his actions while he was in Canada.

Relevant Sections Of The Indian Penal Code (Ipc) Involved

Section 477A (Falsification of Books of Accounts), 420 (Cheating), 471 (Creation of documents for the purpose of cheating by manipulating books of accounts).

Case Study 3: Make Numbers At All Cost

Modus Operandi

Manipulation of Revenue to Attract Retail Investors through IPO

Profit & Loss Account Items involved: Sales inflated by pre-booking & Overvaluation of stock

Balance Sheet items involved: Debtors & Overvaluation of Stock

Company Involved: Ferro Steel (names changed)

Introduction

Ferro Steel was founded by A. B. Tambe, an engineer in the Telecommunication sector, and sold wireless components. Their clients solely included manufacturers for installation into their products. Ram Rao was the CFO of the company. Both of them were over a decade-old friends who worked together previously. Ferro Steel, right from its initial stages, saw dramatic growth. With the addition of B. Kulkarni, a veteran sales leader with international contacts, the company reached new heights and eventually invited private equity investments that shaped the company into an IPO.

Sales Techniques

Tambe, Rao, and Kulkarni realized that branches in Maharashtra, which were under Ms. Shikha, performed well and therefore arranged a meeting with her to get a peek into Shikha's thoughts on what could be done to mimic her success. Shikha mentioned that she guaranteed her clients that they could return the products if they were defective and would provide them credit for future purposes.

She also mentioned that none of her clients returned any products. This was a violation of their sales policies, and it baffled Rao as he clearly understood the accounting implications of these transactions, which the other three failed to realize.

Fraud

a. In order to take the company public, it was agreed that a big auditor firm would have to sign the financials of the company. Due to the exponential growth on the verge of an IPO, the auditors had a heightened level of skepticism, especially in the case of revenue recognition. The auditors found handwritten notes saying "right to return if unable to sell" or "5% additional discounts," which were quickly dismissed by Rao.

b. Unsatisfied with the explanation, the auditors addressed the issue to the Board, which quickly set up an investigation team for the same. It was revealed that purchase orders from companies under Shikha had these problems and therefore called her for an interview, where she mentioned that Tambe, Rao, and Kulkarni were aware of these.

c. The auditors also found emails from Rao to Shikha to push sales and offer them whatever incentives necessary to achieve the target without recording the implications of such transactions. He also used the technique of "slow boating," i.e., sending the orders by the slowest route possible so that the sales get recorded prematurely as the goods leave the warehouse before it is due. They found 290 such transactions that were improperly recorded over three years, which would have to be restarted.

Rao faced the burden of unrealistic expectations of the private investors and used any means necessary to drive up sales. He had forsaken his responsibility as the CFO and adopted a "make numbers at all costs" policy.

Consequences

The Board immediately fired Ram Rao and appointed an interim CFO to restate the financials. Additionally, the company had to postpone the IPO listing indefinitely. The company, Tambe, and Rao would have to deal with a tremendous mess had the misstated financials been submitted to the regulators.

Relevant Sections Of The Indian Penal Code (IPC) Involved

Section 477A (Falsification of Books of Accounts), 420 (Cheating Section), 471 (Creation of documents for the purpose of cheating).

Case Study 4: Sunita's Entry

Modus Operandi: Manipulation of Provisions

Profit & Loss Account Items involved: Manipulation in revenue, Provision for Doubtful Debts, and Bad Debts without any approvals

Balance Sheet items involved: Debtors, Reserves (adding to reserves without booking income)

Company Involved: Vaahan Transportation Services (names changed)

Introduction

Vaahan Transportation Services was founded in the 1960s by R. J. Katyal. The company's business was expanding; however, the company remained a closely held company, and the majority of the financing was debt-based. Sunita Bajaj, in her mid-fifties, was a brilliant, demanding, and intimidating CFO known for her ability to predict the outcome of future uncertainties. She was previously an auditor with a big four company and specialized in the transportation sector. She held a good balance between work and family life.

Fraud

Forensic financial statement analysis typically includes horizontal and vertical relationships between items in the balance sheet, profit and loss account, and cash flows. Therefore, it is important to look at time-sensitive interdependencies to identify possible frauds.

The Internal Auditor, On Analyzing Ten Years Of Data Of The Company, Found That

1. Analysis of provision for doubtful debts showed that in periods of strong revenue growth, the provision had drastically increased, even though the company did a good job at collecting receivables.

2. Many journal entries only had "Sunita's Entry" as an explanation for the entry. Even the head of receivables had no clue as to why these entries were passed.

3. A bad-debts-NA (Not Assigned) ledger was opened where management passed entries to make adjustments. These entries were normally made by Jenny and did not need any other approval.

4. Regulatory reserves were where the contingent liabilities were normally recorded. This ledger also saw drastic increases and decreases over the period of Sunita's instruction.

5. They also found a voucher copy with the copy of an email Jenny sent instructing the accountants not to book income and transfer it to reserves instead.

It became blatantly obvious that Sunita was trying to smooth out the earnings of the company. The reserves were decreased when earnings were low and increased when earnings were high, thereby painting a smooth picture of the financial position of the company.

Consequences

Instead of firing Sunita, the company gave her the option of retiring, which she happily took to spend more time with her family. Additionally, to protect the reputation of the company, the financials were restated, and the legal team began the process of contacting NSE and debt underwriters to inform them about the situation as well as the actions the company would take.

Relevant Sections Of The Indian Penal Code (Ipc) Involved

Section 477A (Falsification of Books of Accounts), 420 (Cheating Section 471), Creation of documents for the purpose of cheating by manipulating books of accounts, 406 (Criminal Breach of Trust).

Case Study 5: Decorating Investor's Dreams

Modus Operandi: Diversion of funds for buying personal assets and siphoning off shareholders' fund

Balance Sheet items involved: Intercorporate Deposits given, Preference Share Capital

Company Involved: Universe Décor Limited (name changed)

Introduction

Universe Décor Limited ("UDL") was a listed company carrying on the plywood business. Galaxy Industries Limited ("GIL") is another listed company carrying on a similar business. Both these companies had a common director, Karan Reddy.

Background

In August 2017, UDL raised INR 270 crores through the issue of preferential equity shares in the open market for the purpose of acquiring the majority of GIL (INR 111 crores) and the balance (INR 159 crores) for business expansion. This acquisition surged the prices of UDL. In October 2017, the company completed the acquisition of GIL. By January 2018, the share prices of UDL were at an all-time high, gaining much confidence from investors at large. GIL raised additional INR 375 crores by April 2018, with its share prices also at an all-time high.

Unfolding of Fraud

1. By March 2019, investors realized that the share prices were following a downward trend. Reddy repeatedly assured the shareholders that the fall in prices is temporary and would rise

back in the near future. By May 2021, the share prices of both companies completely plummeted, and the Stock Exchange banned any further trading in both these companies. On scrutiny of the documents uploaded on the stock exchange, it was found that:

2. Out of INR 159 crores raised, UDL forwarded another INR 130 crores to GIL as inter-company deposits as against the prospectus where UDL were to use these funds for business expansion.

3. GIL passed on INR 260 crores to Star Holding Private Limited ("Star") as advances for the purchase of a property. Reddy held 99.99% shareholding of Star. Star was obligated to transfer the underlying assets in favor of GIL but did not fulfill the said obligation.

4. Public documents of Star revealed that the company had purchased 100% shareholding in an existing SEZ for INR 320 crores. It further revealed that the SEZ was earning income up to INR 60 crores per annum, which was enjoyed solely by the director, Reddy, while both the listed companies continuously posted losses.

Consequences

The preferential equity owners filed a complaint against the director in NCLT. Some interim relief has been received by the shareholders.

Simultaneously, a criminal case has also been filed against Reddy for siphoning off funds of the company and deceiving investors. It was further revealed through an investigation that Reddy already sold his company, namely, Star, to an unknown party to cover up his shortcomings.

Relevant Sections Of The Indian Penal Code (Ipc) Involved

Section 420 (Cheating), 410 (Possessing Stolen Property of the Shareholder's (Company)), 406 (Criminal Breach of Trust of Shareholders), 403 (Dishonest Dealing in Property).

Case Study 6: Undisclosed Bank Account

Modus Operandi: Opening a Bank Account for the benefit of a Division (all employees) remaining unrecorded in books of accounts and siphoning off revenue, fictitious sales

Profit & Loss Account Items involved: Sales (fictitious sales)

Balance Sheet items involved: Bank Account (undisclosed), Debtors (Fictitious party/Shell company)

Other items covered: Weak Internal Control

Company Involved: Perfect Inc. (Name Changed)

Introduction

Perfect Inc. was operating in Texas, and it merged with a similar company in New York. Both the companies were big companies, so there were teething problems immediately after the merger in case of consolidation.

Background

The CEO of Perfect Inc., Mr. Mark, received a call from Melon Bank in New York, asking for some information about the bank account maintained with them by the merged company (the Bank was a small one and was not capable of handling transactions larger than $1 million and also thought it might be the case of money laundering). Mr. Mark inquired with the Treasury and Accounts department to find, to his surprise, that no such account was maintained with such a bank in New York.

Unfolding Of Fraud

- On investigation, it was found that the address in this unknown bank account was that of the Business Unit Controller of the IT unit, Mr. James of the merged company, and also the signatories were the Business Unit Controller, Mr. James, and President of the IT unit, Mr. John.

- Mr. Investigator, one of the team members under the CEO, was sent for further inquiry to New York. On inquiry, he was given an explanation by the IT President that they maintained this account for the benefit of the company.

- The IT unit was the only profitable unit of the merged company; they used to defer the revenue by using this account and transferring revenue/profits to the next period. At the time of the merger, this account was wrongly not included in the bank account list. While going through the transactions in the bank account, Mr. Investigator found names of three parties repeatedly appearing, and on further investigation, he could find that these parties were not on the customer's list.

- Later, he also found out that the telex number written for these parties was not regular and started with IT. Mr. James and Mr. John were called to the Head office in Texas and were just given warnings since Mr. James' unit was the only unit that had performed well after the merger.

- Mr. James and Mr. John were told that there would be proper watch on them in the future, and they were allowed to go. Internal investigators were replaced by external investigators who came with the report after a year, reporting that the bank accounts were maintained for personal gain. The three parties whose dealings could be seen in the account were fictitious parties.

- The sales to such parties were shown only to improve employee bonuses. Almost all employees in the unit had some or the other role to play in it and were all beneficiaries by way of improved bonuses. Sales to fictitious companies were shown, which increased revenue for the company, and employees received incentives for increased sales.

Consequences

External investigations were referred to the Department of Justice. John and James were both fired. John was fined with $5 million and sentenced to one year in prison, and James was fined with $2.5 million. The IT unit had to restate its revenue and file amended income tax returns. The IT's revised financial statements showed losses of $180 million. The IT unit office was closed, and most of the employees were terminated.

Relevant Sections Of The Indian Penal Code (IPC) Involved

Section 420 (Cheating), 410 (Possessing Stolen Property of the Company), 406 (Criminal Breach of Trust of Company Management), 403 (Dishonest Dealing in Property).

Case Study 7: A Super Family Business

Modus Operandi: Misappropriation of company's funds for personal use.

Profit & Loss Account Items involved: Expenses (Booking fictitious Cash Expenses)

Balance Sheet items involved: Cash

Company Involved: Super Enterprises (names changed)

Introduction

Super Enterprises was founded by three brothers, Chintan, Manohar, and Akash Chopra, in the 1950s. Later, over 50% of the companies under this conglomerate were owned by the Chopra Family. Manohar and Akash soon retired and left the operations of the company with Chintan. The retired brothers only signed the financials without going through the same and received their dividends on a regular basis. Jatin Chopra is the son of Chintan and heir to the Super Enterprises group.

Fraud

The retired brothers rarely looked into the affairs of the entity and only met in board meetings for statutory reasons. Chintan realized that he could submit financials without worrying about the board members reviewing them. Consequently, Chintan booked cash expenses in the books of accounts. As time passed, he bought luxurious estates using the company's funds (International Division) and acquired companies abroad, withdrawing huge salaries as President of these companies.

His fortune skyrocketed while the company declined every year. Jatin soon took his father's place on the board and carried out the same fraud that his father had committed.

Unfolding Of Fraud

Jatin's cousin, Mayur, received the financial statements and noticed that there was no mention of his dividend in them. He was left astounded as his dividends had ceased without notice, even though the company was profitable.

After receiving numerous letters from Mayur's lawyers, Jatin agreed to show the books of accounts 21 days before the annual shareholders meeting.

Meanwhile, Mayur's lawyers contacted shareholders who were not being paid dividends as well, amassing over 50% of shareholders. The forensic team was able to find out over 100 violations by studying the older financials which were still with other shareholders. They also found out that all of his new ventures ended in total failure. The financials were not consistent and were presented in a different manner each year.

Consequences

- Mayur and other shareholders got the external auditors' credentials suspended and the practice liquidated.

- They also went to news channels to make the story public, putting pressure on Jatin.

- Consequently, Jatin and Mayur agreed upon a settlement where Jatin bought shares of Super at an agreed-upon rate.

- The option of a trial was not convenient as legal cases would go on for over 20 years, and therefore no dividend would be received by Mayur and the shareholders during the period.

Relevant Sections Of The Indian Penal Code (IPC) Involved

Section 420 (Cheating by recording siphoning off company's funds for buying personal assets), 410 (Possessing Stolen Property of the Company), 406 (Criminal Breach of Trust of Company Management), 403 (Dishonest Dealing in Property).

Case Study 8: Ghost Employees

Modus Operandi: Inflated sales, thus showing a rosy picture (overstated profits) to attract investors, Payment of Salary to a few employees (fictitious persons) in cash and thus misappropriating company's funds, Same internal and external auditor

Profit & Loss Account Items involved: Sales by showing overpriced services to clients & Expenses (by paying ghost employees)

Balance Sheet items involved: Overvaluation of Debtors & Overstating Reserves

Company Involved: Ideal Carriers (names changed)

Introduction

Aditya and Jagmohan Chaudhary were brothers from a well-off family known for never compromising on Integrity for the purpose of prosperity. Chaudhary brothers became financial advisors and soon became experts in identifying loopholes in tax law. After a couple of years of practice, they started a new venture called Ideal Carriers, a transport operator company. After eight years, the company became the largest local carrier.

Due Diligence

On the success of Ideal Carriers, a private equity firm was considering an investment in the company. At first glance, the company was financially strong and profitable. However, on analyzing the ratios, it was found that employee cost to revenue was half of the industry average, and employee retention was 95%. These contradicting ratios raised suspicion. After much digging, it was found that Ideal Carriers were paying a portion of the employee's salary in cash. It was also discovered that approximately 80% of the employees had no trace on the internet, creating a possibility that there were ghost employees. An investigation into the auditors was also conducted, revealing that the internal and external auditors had no previous association with Ideal Carriers. Furthermore, an old annual report written by Aditya and his partner revealed that this person was now a partner in the audit firm employed by Ideal.

A chance encounter with a past colleague surprisingly informed me that the Chaudhary brothers had split their original audit firm into two, run by their trusted employees. These same two firms were now the internal and external auditors of Ideal Carriers. Upon learning about these developments, the private equity firm immediately halted the negotiations.

Fraud

During the same time, the tax and revenue department conducted a raid on Ideal Carriers and its two auditors, revealing a much bigger fraud than anticipated. Aditya floated a sham company, Ideal Carriers, which provided overpriced services to its clients. To legitimize its business, it purchased 50 vehicles. Occasionally, they also helped clients transport goods without having to pay taxes, thus helping them save significant money.

Aditya exaggerated Ideal's volumes and accordingly purchased more fleets and created ghost employees to keep the financial ratios in line with the industry standards. Aditya had identified his clients' desire to avoid paying taxes, not by breaking the law, but by taking full advantage of the existing loopholes.

Consequences

- Chaudhary Brothers' professional certifications were revoked by respective institutes.

- Ideal Carriers were immediately dissolved.

- Aditya was arrested and later granted bail, along with heavy penalties.

- Both audit firms were dissolved.

Relevant Sections Of The Indian Penal Code (Ipc) Involved

Section 420 (Cheating), 410 (Possessing Stolen Property of the Company), 406 (Criminal Breach of Trust of Government), 403 (Dishonest Dealing in Property), 120B (Criminal Conspiracy).

Case Study 9: Speak Asia Ponzi Scheme

Modus Operandi: Collecting web subscriptions, promising annual payment, and transferring money to foreign associates

Profit & Loss Account Items involved: Revenue (High revenue by luring the public to invest)

Balance Sheet items involved: Loans to foreign associates (Related Party Transactions)

Company Involved: Speak Asia Online Limited

Introduction

Speak Asia Online was established in 2006 by Ms. Haren Kaur in Singapore and then expanded to Indonesia and Malaysia. In 2010, Speak Asia was launched in India, in 2011 in Bangladesh, and then in China and the Philippines. It is a Market Research & Survey Company.

Background

Speak Asia was an online survey marketing company that sold web subscriptions for Rs 11,000 each. The investor had to fill out survey forms for multinational firms for a promised annual payment of Rs. 52,000. The company had asked investors or "panellists" to fill in online survey forms every week to earn Rs 52,000 a year. Speak Asia Online Ltd. promised additional commissions if you enrolled more members. The Promoter along with his accomplices, set up a fake company registered in Singapore and set up a pyramid scheme that promised high returns for an initial deposit.

Fraud

a. Speak Asia folded its operation in India in mid-2011, and its senior officials went into hiding after paying a few initial investors. They also started traveling all over the country and acted like tycoons with a lavish lifestyle to encourage their agents to bring more clients into the net.

b. In one such meeting held in Goa, they hired a special train to Goa for the investors, and an exclusive portion of the beach of a resort was booked. The open invitation was attended by many, and leading stars of Bollywood performed in this program. The company duped 24 lakh people to the tune of Rs 2,276 crore. At least eight cases were registered in Mumbai, Andhra Pradesh. Speak Asia remitted Rs 900 crore to Singapore. The money was then sent to Dubai, Italy, and the United Kingdom. Interestingly, the money came back from the United Kingdom again to Dubai and back to India.

Unfolding Of Fraud

a. The Promoters paid the early investors using money collected from newer entrants and continued the cycle until he finally faced investigation over his business practices, and it emerged that he had, meanwhile, duped his investors of a total of about $20 million.

b. Investors filed cases in different states, and the management went hiding. It was later found that the Promoters and his aides took over or set up multi-level marketing companies registered in foreign countries — Ad-Matrix in Singapore and Seven Rings International in Italy, for instance — attracting investments due to their global profile. There were some buyouts in Brazil as well.

c. These were later used to launder money. One such company — Speak Asia in Singapore — was introduced in India in 2010 by the brothers with the help of Manoj Sharma.

Consequences

Some 210 bank accounts containing Rs 142 crore have been frozen. A 5,000-page chargesheet filed against Speak Asia's promoters detailing how unsuspecting investors were lured into parting with hard-earned savings — which cost 2.4 million Indians precious savings.

Relevant Sections Of The Indian Penal Code (Ipc) Involved

Section 420 (Cheating to people at large by luring them to subscribe), 410 (Possessing Stolen Property of the Company), 406 (Criminal Breach of Trust of people at large), 403 (Dishonest Dealing in Property), 120B (Criminal Conspiracy).

Case Study 10: The Story Of India's Biggest Corporate Fraud

Modus Operandi: Diversion of Company's funds to related parties and misappropriation of company's funds for the purchase of personal assets, Overstatement of Bank Balances

Profit & Loss Account Items involved: Revenue (Overstatement by entering fake Sales) & Administrative Expenses (Ghost Employees)

Balance Sheet items involved: Overstatement of Debtors by showing fictitious debtors & Bank Balances

Company Involved: Satyam Computer Services Ltd.

Introduction

Satyam Computer Services Limited is a worldwide IT firm situated in India. Satyam Computer was India's IT crown jewel and the country's fourth-largest company with high-profile customers. In 2007 and 2009, Satyam received the Golden Peacock Award for the best-governed corporation in September 2008.

Mr. Ramalinga Raju established the company in Hyderabad in 1987. The company began with 20 workers and quickly expanded to become a worldwide company with operations in 65 countries across the world. Satyam was the first Indian business to be listed on three global stock exchanges, namely New York Stock Exchange (NYSE), DOW Jones, and EURONEXT.

Background

In the fiscal year 2003-2004, Satyam's total revenues were Rs. 25,415.4 million. By March 2008, the company's sales revenue had increased by more than thrice. Satyam Computers had announced the acquisition of a 100 percent share in Maytas Properties and Maytas Infra, two firms owned by the Chairman's sons. The proposed $1.6 billion purchase was called off seven hours later owing to investor opposition to the buyout.

Fraud

There were multiple types of frauds in the company:

- Inflated the number of employees by 10,000 on January 22, 2009, which enabled the Chairman to withdraw roughly Rs. 20 crores per month from these ghost employees.

- The assets were overvalued by $1.47 billion in the Balance Sheet. The company claimed to hold about $1.04 billion in bank accounts and cash, but none of it existed.

- Over the years, Satyam had inflated income almost every quarter to match the analyst's expectations.

- By claiming interest revenue from the fictitious bank accounts, the Promoter inflated his income statement.

- The company's worldwide head of internal audit established fictitious customer accounts and made fake invoices in their names.

- He had also diverted a large sum of money to other companies that he owned, and he had been doing so since 2004.

Unfolding Of Fraud

The scam was discovered in late 2008 when the Hyderabad property market collapsed, leaving a trail back to Satyam. The scandal was brought to light in 2009 when the Chairman confessed that the company's accounts had been falsified.

Consequences

- Under the Indian Penal Code, 1860, the accused were charged with criminal breach of trust, cheating, criminal conspiracy, and forgery. Satyam's board was reformed by the Central Government.

- Satyam's auditors PricewaterhouseCoopers (PwC), ultimately stated that their audit report was incorrect because it was based on incorrect financial statements submitted by Satyam's management, a week after Satyam founder's sensational confession.

- Andhra Pradesh State CB-CID had raided the house of the founders relatives', who owned 4.3 percent of Maytas Infra. One hundred twelve sale deeds of different land purchases and development agreements were recovered from the house.

- Satyam's clients reported a lack of faith in the company and reassessed their contracts, opting to deal with other rivals instead.

- Satyam's contracts with Cisco, Telstra, and the World Bank were all canceled.

- Shareholders lost their money.

- Bankers were worried about the recovery of Loans.

Relevant Sections Of The Indian Penal Code (Ipc) Involved

Section 420 (Cheating), 468 (Forgery), 409 (Criminal Breach of Trust), 120B (Criminal Conspiracy).

References

www.hindustantimes.com

www.financialexpress.com

www.thehindubusinessline.com

Case Study 11: Nirav Modi Scam

Modus Operandi: Fake Letter of Undertaking to raise money overseas

Balance Sheet items involved: Bank Loan

Notes to Accounts items involved: Contingent Liabilities (Bank Guarantees)

Company Involved: Firestar Diamond International, Gitanjali Group

Introduction

Nirav Modi is a luxury diamond jeweler and designer who was ranked 57th in the Forbes list of billionaires in 2017. He is also the founder of the Nirav Modi chain of diamond jewelry retail stores. Modi is the Chairman of Firestar International, the parent of the Nirav Modi chain, which has stores in key markets across the globe. He has 16 stores in diverse locations, such as Delhi, Mumbai, New York, Hong Kong, London, and Macau.

Background

The whole scam took place with LoU (Letter of Undertaking), which is a form of bank guarantee. It allows the LoU receiver to raise money overseas by showing the LoU. The foreign banks (overseas branches of Indian Banks) see the LoU and give credit/loan to the debtor, and the bank giving the LoU stays as a guarantee that in case the debtor fails to repay the debt, the bank will repay the same. Also, a credit limit is sanctioned by the bank giving LoU. Thus, LoUs gave cheap buyer's credit for short-term purposes.

Fraud

Bankers used fake Letters of Undertakings (LoUs) at PNB's Brady House branch in Fort Mumbai. The LoUs were opened in favor of branches of Indian banks for the import of pearls for a period of one year, for which Reserve Bank of India guidelines lay out a total time period of 90 days from the date of shipment.

All these LoU transactions were not added to the PNB's Core Banking System (CBS), which is used for record-keeping purposes. All these unauthorized LoU-related transactions were done by corrupt officials using the SWIFT system, an elaborate messaging network used by banks and financial institutions internationally to accurately, quickly, and safely send and receive financial information. The SWIFT system had no linkage with the bank's record-keeping core system, i.e., CBS, and this gave the perpetrators the shadow area to operate with unauthorized LoUs. Since the overseas Indian bank branches trusted their Indian counterparts without scrutinizing the credit quality, they promptly issued loans (buyer's credit) to these firms.

Unfolding Of Fraud

When one of the corrupt officials retired, a new official was appointed in his place. But this official asked for collateral from these firms for granting LoUs as per the norms, upon which he was told that these firms are used to getting LoUs without collateral for many years. Also, the foreign banks which had given loans to them based on PNB's LoUs came knocking at the doors of PNB. At this juncture, internal investigations had started, but no records of such transactions were found because the bank officials did not keep relevant records of the unauthorized LoUs in the bank's CBS (Core Banking System).

On January 29, 2018, PNB lodged an FIR with CBI stating that fraudulent LoUs worth Rs 2.8 billion (Rs 280.7 crore) were first issued on January 16. In the complaint, PNB had named three diamond firms, Diamonds R Us, Solar Exports, and Stellar Diamonds. As of May 18, 2018, the scam came out to over Rs 14,000 crore.

Consequences

- All the accused parties escaped India in early 2018, days before the news of the scam became public.

- CBI issued arrest warrants against the two corrupt employees of PNB and executives of these firms who were integral to the scam.

- The Enforcement Directorate (ED) seized diamonds, gold, and jewelry items from the perpetrators home, shops, and offices worth Rs.56.74 billion (approx).

- Bankruptcy proceedings were filed by Firestar Diamond International, in the United States.

- Interpol issued a Red Corner Notice against the accused for money laundering and fraud.

- A Mumbai Court issued an order against them to appear before the Court or be declared fugitives as per the provisions of the Prevention of Money Laundering Act (PMLA), 2002.

Relevant Sections Of The Indian Penal Code (IPC) Involved

Section 420 (Cheating and dishonestly inducing delivery of property), 409 (Criminal Breach of Trust by Public Servants (Bankers)), 120B (Criminal Conspiracy).

References

www.business-standard.com

www.thehindu.com

www.economictimes.indiatimes.com

Case Study 12: Ricoh India Accounting Fraud

Modus Operandi: Diversion and Siphoning off funds, falsification of accounts, and Window Dressing

Balance Sheet items involved: Debtors and Stock (inventory)

Profit & Loss Account items involved: Sales, closing stock, Provision for Doubtful Debts

Company Involved: Ricoh India Limited

Introduction

Ricoh India Limited is a company incorporated as a joint venture between RPG Industries and Ricoh Japan in 1993. Ricoh is the manufacturer of office automation equipment and manufactures copiers and facsimile machines.

Fraud

The issues highlighted in the forensic audit report ordered by SEBI are as follows:

1. Revenue from the sale of goods was recorded without the goods being delivered in many cases.

2. Revenue from service contracts was recorded on invoicing instead of the company's practice of recording revenue on the percentage of completion method.

3. Unsupported out-of-book adjustments of Rs. 66.7 crores were made in the quarter ended 30th September 2015, converting a loss of Rs. 64.0 crores to a profit of Rs. 2.67 crores and thereby inflating the reserves too.

4. Inflated inventories were shown by Rs. 118 crores, and inflated receivables to the tune of Rs. 446.4 crores were shown in books resulting in an inflated reserve position amounting to Rs. 564.6 crores.

5. Some back-to-back sales and purchase transactions were done with 18 entities just to meet the forecast.

6. Goods delivered were shown to fake addresses, and multiple inconsistencies were found in business addresses or email addresses of certain parties. Sales amounting to Rs. 418 crores were shown to these non-existent/non-traceable 13 select parties. Some parties were interrelated in terms of common directorships, etc.

7. The majority of suspect transactions were recorded at the end of the month and were recorded backdated to meet the sales target.

8. Write-offs were made in the Annual financial statements of F.Y. 2015-16 on account of non-recovery of debtors and non-existent inventories.

9. One party called FDSL - with which Ricoh had transactions of purchase and sales - was a major write-off during 12-13 to 16-17. On further investigation, it was found that frequent amounts were paid to this company, and from the bank statements of FDSL, it was found that immediate amounts were transferred to two companies where KMP of Ricoh or their spouses were shareholders and directors. Thus, funds were siphoned off/ diverted for the benefit of KMPs.

Unfolding Of Fraud

In July 2015, the Statutory auditors of Ricoh were changed, and Ricoh failed to publish quarter two results. The new auditors pointed out financial irregularities, and BSE moved Ricoh shares to the "z" category. SEBI appointed forensic auditors, and MD & CEO CFO, and COO were sent on paid leave. Ricoh filed a police complaint against six officials. A loss of Rs. 1,123 crores was incurred due to fudged accounts.

Consequences

Ricoh Japan, the parent company, infused Rs. 1,123 crores into Ricoh India in 2016. Its top executives took a 15% pay cut due to the huge losses incurred in the Indian business.

Relevant Sections Of The Indian Penal Code (IPC) Involved

Section 420 (Cheating), 120B (Criminal Conspiracy),
477A (Falsification of Accounts).

References

www.economictimes.indiatimes.com, www.livemint.com

Case Study 13: Expensive Cup Of Coffee

Modus Operandi: Siphoning off Company funds for buying personal property through related party transactions

Balance Sheet items involved: Loans given to Related Party for siphoning off money to buy personal property & Bank Loans

Company Involved: Café Coffee Day

Introduction

Café Coffee Day (CCD) is a multinational chain of coffee houses having its headquarters in Bengaluru, Karnataka. V. G. Siddhartha started the café chain in 1996 when he incorporated Coffee Day Global, which is the parent of the Coffee Day chain and in the business of growing coffee in its own estate of 20,000 acres. The company did vertical integration as per the strategy to cut costs: from owning the plantations to growing coffee, making the coffee machine, and making the furniture for the outlets.

Fraud

Café Coffee Day was shaken by the suspected suicide of its founder V.G. Siddhartha in 2019. A subsequent investigation found Siddhartha had routed Rs. 2700 crores ($360m) out of the company through transactions revealed in a note found after his death.

Unfolding Of Fraud

The investigation took place, and the report revealed that Mysore Amalgamated Coffee Estates Limited (MACEL) – the private company once held by Siddhartha -- owes Rs 3,535 crore to the subsidiaries of Coffee Day Enterprises as on July 31, 2019. However, according to the Consolidated Audited Financial Statements of the company, MACEL owed only Rs 842 crore to subsidiaries as on March 31, 2019, thus revealing a gap of Rs 2,693 crore that indicates a scam.

MACEL is a private coffee trading firm that was owned by Siddhartha and his father. The report suggested that the missing Rs 2,693 crore may have been transferred by Siddhartha to his company, possibly to pay back investors, repay loans or even fund his other private investments.

Since this was outside the scope of the investigation, the report did not account for it; the report has just pointed out the whopping missing amount. In a disclosure to the stock exchanges, the board of Coffee Day said that the company's subsidiaries are taking steps to recover dues from MACEL.

Consequences

Mr. V. G. Siddhartha committed suicide and, in the suicide note, VGS had said, "The law should hold me and only me accountable, as I have withheld the information from everybody, including my family."

In March 2020, Coffee Day Enterprises Limited announced that it had reached an agreement to sell Global Village Technology Park, a 90-acre tech park on the outskirts of Bengaluru, for a total consideration of ₹2,700 crore for repaying the debt of Cafe Coffee Day's associate firms and their promoters.

CDEL, which was facing debts of ₹7,200 crores, is pairing its debts by disposing of assets and now brought down to ₹3,200 crores, and would bring it further down as it plans to sell more assets.

Relevant Sections Of The Indian Penal Code (IPC) Involved

Section 421 (Fraudulent removal or concealment of property to prevent distribution among creditors), 120B (Criminal Conspiracy).

References

www.livemint.com

www.indiatoday.in

www.timesnownews.com

Case Study 14: King Of Good Times

Modus Operandi: Diversion of funds to associates, misappropriation of company's funds for buying personal property

Balance Sheet items involved: Loans to related parties & Loans from Banks

Company Involved: Kingfisher Airlines

Introduction

In 2005, Vijay Mallya launched 'Kingfisher Airlines' which was known for its luxury travels. Soon it became the 2nd largest airline in the domestic market, having 1/4th of India's share of domestic travelers. To expand, he also acquired Air Deccan.

He concentrated only on expansion and not on profits. Hence he took loans. The market share of Kingfisher started decreasing, and the burden of debt started increasing (one of the reasons was the acquisition of Air Deccan). FDI was not allowed in the aviation sector then. Thus, eventually, the government canceled its license in 2012. Loans were taken from 17 Banks; the majority were PSUs. In March 2016 loans outstanding was Rs. 9,000 crores with interest.

Fraud

In 2011, Kingfisher abruptly canceled 35 flights, for which DCGA asked an explanation. The management replied to this as a well-planned restructuring. Suppliers were pressurizing for payments or warning to stop the supplies. Kingfisher was not paying the employees on a timely basis, and the news came in July 2011. Almost 24 pilots and a few crew members left the company in November 2011. Kingfisher failed in payment of taxes and loan repayments.

Unfolding Of Fraud

a. Forensic auditor E & Y appointed by SBI found diversion of funds by Kingfisher to Formula One, a company of Vijay Mallya and other ventures of promoter Vijay Mallya. The airline was also being investigated for suspected diversion of funds and financial irregularities. An account was created in HDFC bank, from where the company was siphoning off money.

b. The Enforcement Directorate (ED) alleged that Kingfisher Airlines diverted Rs 3,547 crore of the loan granted by a consortium of 17 lenders. It over-invoiced the lease rentals of aircraft between April 2008 and March 2012 to the extent of Rs. 3432.40 crores and diverted Rs. 45.42 crores for making a payment towards the rental lease of a corporate jet which was used exclusively by the Promoter. Diversion of Rs. 50.90 crores from Kingfisher Airlines to Force Indian Formula One Team. Diversion of Rs 15.90 crores to his own firm that owned IPL team Royal Challengers Bangalore. Rs. 2.78 crores for payment of old ICICI Bank loan.

c. Detailing the misrepresentation, the agency has said that Kingfisher obtained loans from banks and transferred the funds to its bank account in London on the pretext of "making local payments in the United Kingdom" for "fuel, airport charges, hotel expenditure, and other operating expenses" in connection with their flights there. However, the ED found that Rs 50.90 crore transferred to the London account of the airlines was diverted to Force One Formula One Team.

d. The ED has alleged that he "has amassed huge properties outside India, especially in United Kingdom, USA, France, and other countries" and "has got interested in various companies which are created/incorporated outside India." "These facts of overseas properties and companies have not been mentioned in the asset/liability statement submitted and have been deliberately hidden from the banks."

Consequences

a) He was accused of fraud and money laundering in the country.

b) The accused fled to the UK in 2016

c) ED has accused Kingfisher Airlines and Promoter of money laundering and said they are involved in "concealment, possession, acquisition and use of proceeds of crime."

d) The accused has been declared a proclaimed offender by a special Prevention of Money Laundering Act (PMLA) court and is currently fighting extradition in the UK.

e) Based in Britain for over five years, he is pursuing appeals in the UK courts in an attempt to overturn a bankruptcy order imposed on him by the High Court in London in July 2021.

Relevant Section Of Indian Penal Code (IPC) Involved

Section 420 (Cheating), 120B (Criminal Conspiracy).

References

www.economictimes.indiatimes.com

www.business-standard.com

www.thehindu.com

Case Study 15: Rotomac Fraud Case

Modus Operandi: Siphoning off funds through payments to fictitious overseas suppliers (Shell companies)

Profit & Loss Account items involved: Purchases (purchases from Fictitious overseas suppliers) & Sales (sales to fictitious overseas buyers)

Balance Sheet items involved: Debtors (Fictitious parties) & Creditors (Fictitious parties), Bank Loans

Company Involved: Rotomac Global Pvt. Ltd. (Formerly known as Rotomac Pen Pvt. Ltd.)

Introduction

Vikram Kothari, the promoter of Rotomac Pen Pvt. Ltd., came from the family of founders of Pan Parag Paan Masala. Rotomac Pen Pvt. Ltd. was formed in 1992. Rotomac emerged as a top player in the writing instruments market. Top Bollywood actors were the brand ambassadors. Later, the company name was changed to Rotomac Global Pvt. Ltd., and Vikram Kothari moved into sectors like real estate, steel, and infrastructure.

Fraud

Between 2008 to 2013, the Promoters moved to defraud seven public sector banks by getting foreign letters of credit (FLCs) for making payments to overseas suppliers having offices in Dubai, Sharjah, Hongkong. Total exposure to banks was around Rs. 3,700 crores.

Unfolding Of Fraud

The money was round-tripped to accounts of Rotomac and its sister concerns. Some examples of round-tripping by Rotomac are

a) Rs. 15.50 crores packing credit disbursed in the current account of the company for executing export orders, out of which Rs. 3 crores were remitted to the company's other accounts immediately.

b) Rs. 34 crore packing credit disbursed for executing export orders to a company in Singapore. This money was transferred to one Bargadia Brothers Pvt. Ltd. and from them Rs. 16 crores back to Rotomac account immediately.

Incomplete documents were produced for trades, and that too only photocopies on the pretext that the originals were sent to the importer.

When Bank of Baroda executives personally visited Dubai, Sharjah, and Hongkong suppliers/buyers, either the office was closed, or it was only a virtual office. Thus, the import/export business was with shell companies.

Consequences

The bank alleged that the Promoter and the company had violated the Foreign Exchange Management Act and worked for interest rate differentials in local and foreign currency in the name of trade without any genuine business transactions. CBI filed FIR against the Rotomac scam of Rs. 3,695 crores

Relevant Sections Of The Indian Penal Code (IPC) Involved

Section 420 (Cheating and dishonesty including delivery of property), 467 (Forgery of valuable security, will, etc.), 468 (Forgery for the purpose of cheating), 471 (Using a genuine forged document/ electronic record), 120B (Criminal Conspiracy).

References

www.timesofindia.indiatimes.com

www.business-standard.com

www.thehindu.com

Case Study 16: India's Biggest Bank Fraud

Modus Operandi: Related Party Transactions + Acquisition of assets in overseas related parties

Balance Sheet items involved: Loans to related parties (98 companies were floated) & Loans from Banks

Company Involved: ABG Shipyard Ltd.

Introduction

The Gujarat-based ABG Shipyard, incorporated in 1985 - once a key player in shipbuilding and ship repair - is the flagship company of the ABG Group. Its shipyards - located in Gujarat's Dahej and Surat - have built over 165 vessels in the last 16 years. Forty-six of these ships were for export. Mr. Rishi Kamla Agarwal is the chairman of the company.

Fraud

a. From 2012 to 2017 (5 years), ABG Shipyard defrauded 28 banks for Rs. 23,000 crore debt. Loans were given to these companies from 2005 to 2010, and fraud occurred from 2012 to 2017. Money was transferred to One Ocean Shipping Company Pvt. Ltd. and ABG Engineering & Construction Ltd. – these entities transferred them to another company called PFS Shipping India Ltd. PFS Shipping then allegedly adjusted the receivables to ABG SL.

b. According to Master Restructuring Agreement, ABG SL should have recovered an investment of Rs 236 crore made by its subsidiary ABG Shipyard Singapore in the units of Standard Chartered Trust within two months from the date of Corporate

Debt Reconstruction. Instead, ABG SL allegedly invested US$ 43 million in ABG Singapore, which was then potentially diverted.

c. The company had sought permission to invest in overseas subsidiaries, which is a general business practice. But a huge chunk was re-routed for some other purpose other than what was declared. It is also suspected that this money may be diverted to tax havens.

d. During the financial year 2014-15, ABG SL had paid accommodation deposits worth Rs 83 crores in total to companies-related entities like Aries Management Services, GC Properties, and Gold Croft Properties before the review period (in 2007-08). These companies acquired fixed assets such as property with the security deposits provided by ABG SL in the same year.

e. Rs 95 crore might have been bought in via circular transaction in April 2014 as outflow to linked parties and inflow from ABG International on the same date; the management of the company says the global crisis of 2008 impacted the company a lot. The company's accounts became NPA in 2013. The core business of the company was hit the most, and losses started mounting.

Unfolding Of Fraud

a. EY conducted a forensic audit in January 2019. Fraud was conducted through the diversion of funds, misappropriation, and criminal breach of trust, with an objective to gain unlawfully at the cost of the bank's funds.

b. CBI found out that 98 companies were floated to divert funds.

c. Thus, the fraud is primarily on account of a huge transfer by M/s ABG Shipyard Ltd to its related parties and subsequently making adjustment entries. It is also alleged that huge investments were made in its overseas subsidiary by diverting bank loans.

d. This is a complex scam that involves circular transactions and use by shell companies to layer them. The loans were availed mainly either for the purpose of evergreening of the loans or to create assets for the accused," said an official privy to the development.

Consequences

a) An FIR was registered on February 2, 2022, following an analysis of the basic facts, scrutiny, and discreet verification of the issues mentioned in the complaint.

b) Thirteen locations were searched on February 12, 2022, which led to the discovery of several incriminating documents.

c) A separate money-laundering investigation has also been started against them by the Enforcement Directorate (ED).

Relevant Sections Of The Indian Penal Code (IPC) Involved

Section 420 (Cheating), 406 (Criminal Breach of Trust), 120B (Criminal Conspiracy).

References

www.economictimes.indiatimes.com

www.ndtv.com

www.thehindu.com

Case Study 17: Dishonesty does not give Power

Modus Operandi: Taking loans and defrauding lenders by diverting money to related parties

Balance Sheet items involved: Loans to related parties & Loans from Banks

Company Involved: Bhushan Power & Steel Ltd.

Introduction

Bhushan Power & Steel Ltd. was founded in 1970 and incorporated in 1999 manufacturing Tor Steel and wire rod. Mr. Sanjay Singal promoted the company.

Fraud

a. BPSL, its directors, and staff "dishonestly and fraudulently" diverted ₹ 2,348 crores into the account of various companies showing as advances between April 1, 2007, to March 31, 2014, without any obvious purposes and thereby misused funds.

b. The company and its directors deliberately defaulted in repayment of the loan amount to lender banks as per the time scheduled, and their accounts remained continuously irregular.

c. These proceeds of crime were laundered by way of infusion in the form of equity in BPSL creation of assets in the name of self or his family members directly or indirectly.

Unfolding Of Fraud

a. The ED had initiated its investigation under PMLA on the basis of an FIR filed by CBI on April 5, 2019, against Bhushan Steel and others for a criminal conspiracy with unknown public servants of banks and others to cheat banks and financial institutions.

b. It has been alleged that the firm was used by the Promoter to fraudulently divert huge amounts of bank funds through companies, shell companies, and entities. They did not use the bank loans for the purpose for which they were sanctioned, committed forgery for the purpose of cheating, used forged documents, and falsified the accounts, causing wrongful loss to the lending banks, financial institutions, government exchequer and corresponding wrongful gain to themselves.

c. According to the ED, its investigation has revealed that all accused, diverted huge amounts of funds out of loans taken by Bhushan Steel from 33 banks and financial institutions between 2007 and 2014. These funds were used for creating assets (including equity investment in BPSL and movable and immovable properties in Delhi and London) in the name of companies controlled by .the Promoters.

d. ED had provisionally attached proceeds of crime valued at Rs 204.31 crore in the form of immovable properties belonging to the group companies under the control of the Promoters. The attached assets consist of movable and immovable properties in Delhi and London.

Consequences

In its chargesheet, the ED has named the Promoters & MD of Bhushan Steel, as the main conspirator behind the fraud.

Relevant Sections Of The Indian Penal Code (Ipc) Involved

Section 420 (Cheating), 468 (Forgery for the purpose of cheating), 471 (Use of Forged documents as genuine), 477A (Falsification of Accounts), 168 (Criminal misconduct by public servant), 120B (Criminal Conspiracy).

References

www.economictimes.indiatimes.com

www.indiatoday.in

www.ndtv.com

Case Study 18: All that shines are not Diamonds

Modus Operandi: Exposures taken on Letters of credit, round-tripping, related party transactions

Profit & Loss Account items involved: Sales (Fictitious export invoices and raising letter of credits to borrow from banks)

Balance Sheet items involved: Fake Debtors (overseas related parties) & Loans from Banks

Company Involved: Winsome Diamonds & Jewellery Ltd.

Introduction

In 1985 Mr. Jatin Mehta incorporated a company named Winsome Diamonds & Jewellery Ltd. and Su-Raj Diamonds. He was the founder of the first public diamond trading company in India.

Fraud

The credit limits were granted in the form of standby letters of credit (Letters of credit are guarantees given by the issuing bank that if the client fails to pay, they will pay). The Promoters raised a letter of credit worth Rs. 4,687 crores in seven related companies, including Winsome Diamonds.

A Bank consortium led by Standard Chartered Bank provided these loans in tranches from 2009 to 2012, which were through an overseas order from UAE companies. In 2012 Mehta showed his inability to repay these loans as a big customer from UAE was hit by losses and unable to pay him.

Unfolding Of Fraud

In 2013 and 2014, many FIRs were filed by lenders against the company and its Promoters. CBI investigations went on for three years, but no arrest happened.

In 2015 Winsome Group filed cases in Sharjah Court against the buyers there, and the judgment was in favor of Winsome Group (i.e., the defaults were due to commercial situations for getting overexposed to the credit risk of a few buyers).

Fraud was discovered by a Tel-Aviv-based media house. The findings were:

a. Company was raising fictitious export invoices for raising finance

b. Exports proceeds were never recovered in India.

c. Out of 13 distributors in UAE, 12 were controlled by one person who was shown as a part of the Winsome group in insurance papers.

d. Out of these 12, five of them were incorporated on the same date, 15th June 2012.

e. An ED investigation into Winsome Diamonds found that the company allegedly diverted at least $ 750 million (Rs 5,175 crore) to six entities in Hong Kong, Bahamas, and UAE, directly or indirectly controlled by its Promoter, through a web of "dummy companies."

f. Several entities of the group were carrying round tripping of transactions.

Consequences

a. Total defaulted amount of loan is around Rs.8000 crores, owed to 15 banks in India, as per information available in the public domain

b. NCLT had ordered the liquidation of Winsome Diamonds in August 2020, which is pending completion.

c. The creditors of Winsome, mainly banks, are likely to take a haircut of 98 per cent since the diamond firm has assets of only about Rs 200 crore in its balance sheet that can be liquidated, as per press reports

d. The banks were left with nothing. The collateral security provided by Winsome is worth just about Rs 250 crore.

e. Enforcement Directorate (ED) is probing the promoters and the management of Winsome Diamonds and its subsidiaries under the Prevention of Money Laundering Act (PMLA) to establish the money trail that led to the alleged fraud

f. The Promoter, Winsome Diamonds, and its subsidiaries are also being investigated by the Central Bureau of Investigation (CBI) and the Serious Fraud Investigation Office (SFIO).

g. CBI has failed to get an Interpol red notice against the Promoter, who is still absconding

Relevant Sections Of The Indian Penal Code (Ipc) Involved

Section 420 (Cheating), 120B (Criminal Conspiracy).

References

www.economictimes.indiatimes.com

www.thehindubusinessline.com

www.indianexpress.com

Case Study 19: In Your Losses, Lies Our Success

Modus Operandi: Money laundering through shell companies, embezzlement, siphoning off funds

Balance Sheet items involved: Loans to related parties & Loans from Banks

Company Involved: Religare Enterprise Ltd. and Religare Finvest Ltd.

Introduction

Religare Enterprises Ltd's (REL) was promoted by Malvinder and Shivinder Mohan Singh (Singh brothers) as an umbrella company to carry out NBFC, insurance, and other such businesses.

Fraud

a. The Promoters laundered Rs 2,100 crore along with an employee of REL subsidiary, RFL funds, borrowed from banks. The agency said the promoters and the said employee used 19 shell companies to launder the funds.

b. Some of that money was allegedly siphoned off to foreign entities.

c. The Promoters also colluded with the employees of Lakshmi Vilas Bank (LVB) and embezzled two FDs (fixed deposits) of Rs 400 crore and Rs 350 crore made with the bank by RFL (all this happened in 2016)

d. Religare and RFL had cheated, and properties worth "hundreds of crores have been misappropriated, siphoned and diverted through a web of complicated financial transactions."

Unfolding Of Fraud

a. The case was registered on a complaint by a senior Religare manager, who had also been named a stockbroker and an associate of the Promoters.

b. The FIR was lodged on a complaint by RFL which had accused the Promoters of siphoning off funds and diverting loans extended by RFL.

c. The Promoters misappropriated the money by availing loan from the bank against the two FDs in RHC Holdings Pvt. Ltd., a company they owned, and further squared off their liabilities.

Consequences

a. The ED arrested the Promoters.

b. ED registered a money laundering case against the Promoters based on an FIR registered by the Economic Offences Wing of the Delhi Police (EOW).

c. Bail application of the Promoters were rejected.

Relevant Section Of Indian Penal Code (IPC) Involved

Section 420 (Cheating), 406 (Criminal breach of trust), 477A (Falsification of Accounts), 120B (Criminal Conspiracy),

References

www.economictimes.indiatimes.com

www.business-standard.com

www.ndtv.com

Case Study 20: Experience Change

Modus Operandi: Siphoning off Money

Balance Sheet items involved: Loans to related parties & Loans from Banks

Company Involved: Videocon Industries Ltd.

Introduction

Videocon Industries Ltd. controlled by Mr. Dhoot. He also was a 99% shareholder of Supreme Energy Pvt. Ltd., incorporated in July 2008. In January 2019, Nupower Renewables Pvt. Ltd. was incorporated, having Mr. Deepak Husband of CEO of the Banker), Mr. Dhoot, and Mr. Saurabh as first Directors.

Fraud

Total loans given to Videocon group was Rs. 3,250 crores from 2009 to 2011, out of which Loans of Rs. 1,875 was in question due to becoming NPA (out of the same one loan of Rs. 300 crore – details given below)

On September 7, 2009, this loan was dispensed to VIEL.

On the following day, September 8, 2009, Mr. Dhoot transferred Rs 64 crore to Nupower Renewables, managed by Mr. Deepak.

The loan was transferred to Nupower Renewables from Videocon Industries, through Supreme Energy.

This, as per the CBI, was the first major capital received by Nupower Renewables to get its first power plant.

Bank's CEO committed the mistake of not revealing to the bank's board about her husband's other business associations with the Videocon group, which was a customer of the bank. She kept on being a part of the advisory groups that sanctioned credit facilities to Videocon when she should have separated herself on-premise of conflict of interest.

The loans were later converted into NPA.

Unfolding Of Fraud

a. In October 2016, after an investor in both the lender Bank and Videocon Group raised questions via a blog, the topic of suspected loan irregularities came to light. He wrote that the bank's CEO influenced the Venugopal Videocon group's Rs 3,250-crore loan in 2012 in exchange for a contract with NuPower Renewables and Supreme Energy, a renewable energy business owned by her husband, Mr. Deepak.

b. The bank's board additionally communicates full confidence in the CEO, denying any bad behavior on her part and precluding any 'irreconcilable situation'

c. In March 2018, the case again came into the spotlight when another anonymous informant complained against the bank and its top administration, including the CEO, alleging an intentional delay in recognizing hindrance in 31 loan accounts somewhere in the range of 2008 and 2016 to save money on provisioning costs. These charges led to probes by numerous agencies, including the Central Bureau of Investigation (CBI), enforcement directorate (ED), and Serious Fraud Investigation Office (SFIO), and furthermore, questioning of the CEO's relatives.

d. In April 2018, the Serious Fraud Investigation Office (SFIO) sought the nod from the Ministry of Corporate Affairs to check the Rs 3,250 crore loan from the Bank to the Videocon group in 2012.

e. Show cause notice by SEBI to the bank's CEO

f. In the Videocon loan case, the panel of judges found that the CEO infringed the code of conduct of the bank.

g. Dhoot is alleged to have invested in the Nupower organization of Mr. Deepak through his company Supreme Energy, a compensation or quid pro quo for loans cleared by the lender Bank following her taking over as the CEO of the bank.

Consequences

a. The CEO resigned from the Bank (was later treated as dismissal).

b. Central Bureau of Investigation filed an FIR against the CEO, her better half Mr. Deepak, leader of the Videocon group Mr. Dhoot and Bank officials for sanction of credit facilities infringing upon rules, that caused a loss of ₹1,730 crores to the bank.

c. All three were under arrest, but the Bank's CEO and Mr. Dhoot got bail.

Relevant Sections Of The Indian Penal Code (IPC) Involved

Section 420 (Cheating), 120B (Criminal Conspiracy).

References

www.economictimes.indiatimes.com

www.livemint.com

www.indianexpress.com

Case Study 21: All That Glitters Is Not Gold

Modus Operandi: Falsified stock records and documents, misappropriation of company funds for buying personal property

Profit & Loss Account items involved: Closing Stock (falsely shown)

Balance Sheet items involved: Closing Stock (falsely shown) & Loans from Banks

Company Involved: Kanishk Gold Pvt. Ltd.

Introduction

Kanishk Gold Pvt. Ltd. having its registered office at Chennai was is owned and controlled by Bhupesh Kumar Jain and wife Neeta Jain. It was incorporated in 2006 and started taking loans from 2007 to 2012. In 2012 it entered into a consortium agreement with 14 private and public banks.

Fraud

In 2012, it entered into a consortium agreement with 14 private and public banks and took loans amounting to Rs. 824 crores. It was granted a metal gold loan to purchase gold from nominated banks or from the open market. Credit facilities were secured by securities such as raw materials, semi-finished goods, finished goods, stores, and spares, and by showing huge stocks.

Kanishk defaulted on interest payments in March 2017 to 8 member banks. In April 2017, it stopped payment to all 14 banks. The bankers were unable to contact the promoter. In May 2017, when bankers visited Kanishk's corporate office, factory, and showroom, the facilities were shut, with no activity and stock.

Unfolding Of Fraud

An FIR was registered based on a complaint by the General Manager of State Bank of India, Chennai, alleging offenses of forgery, cheating, and criminal conspiracy against the accused.

According to the Forensic Audit report, there has been misrepresentation/falsification of records, diversion of funds, and disposal of stocks by the company.

The total loss caused to banks was to the tune of Rs. 824 crore outstanding as on December 31, 2017.

During the investigation, it was revealed that the Promoters had purchased immovable properties, both in his name and in the name of the company, from bank borrowings. The immovable properties were subsequently mortgaged to the banks in the consortium to avail more credit facilities.

Consequences

The Promoters are not in judicial custody. The ED has now attached 14 such properties belonging to them and their company valued at Rs. 281 crores.

Relevant Sections Of The Indian Penal Code (Ipc) Involved

Section 420 (Cheating), 465 (Forgery (showing forged records of stock, property)), 120B (Criminal Conspiracy).

References

www.timesofindia.indiatimes.com

www.businesstoday.com

www.thehindu.com

Case Study 22: Sandesara Brothers Scam

Modus Operandi: Diversion and Siphoning off funds by opening 174 shell companies

Balance Sheet items involved: Loans to shell companies and then using money for buying personal properties & Loans from Banks

Company Involved: Sterling Biotech Group

Introduction

Sterling Biotech is a Gujrat based pharmaceutical group, Sandesara Group of company. Its main promoters are Nitin Sandesara, Chetan Sandesara, and Deepti Sandesara.

Fraud

Overseas companies of Sandesara group took loans of around Rs.9,000 crores from foreign branches of Indian banks. Sterling Biotech group had obtained loans from Indian banks as well as from foreign branches of Indian Banks.

One hundred seventy-four shell companies were opened by the group in India and abroad. "Funds obtained from loans were diverted for non-mandated purposes, layered and laundered through a web of multiple domestic as well as offshore entities," according to the ED.

Unfolding Of Fraud

The ED registered a case after the Central Bureau of Investigation lodged an FIR in October 2017 on account of cheating and bank fraud to the tune of Rs. 5383 crores against the said company and its promoters (later, the amount of fraud was calculated as Rs. 14,700 crores).

During the investigation, it was found out that the main promoters had not only siphoned off loan funds to finance their Nigerian oil business but also for their personal purposes.

Consequences

A chargesheet against 195 people was made by the ED.

The total attachment, in this case, stands at ₹ 14,543 crores, out of the proceeds of crime of more than ₹ 14,690.95 crores.

All the Promoters and aides have been declared fugitives under the Fugitive Economic Offenders Act by a special PMLA court in Mumbai (as they all ran away to Nigeria)

Relevant Section Of Indian Penal Code (Ipc) Involved

Section 420 (Cheating), 120B (Criminal Conspiracy)

References

www.economictimes.indiatimes.com

www.ndtv.com

www.businesstoday.in

Case Study 23: Mammoth Fraud of Rs. 1 Lakh Crores

Modus Operandi: Diversion and Siphoning off funds by opening 350 subsidiaries

Balance Sheet items involved: Loans to related parties & Loans from Banks

Company Involved: IL&FS Group

Introduction

Infrastructure Leasing & Financial Services Limited (IL&FS) was formed in 1987 by HDFC, UTI and Central Bank of India. The vision of the company is to provide funding to major infrastructure projects across India in multiple segments like transportation, urban infrastructure, education, tourism, etc.

Fraud

IL&FS Financial Services gave huge loans for long-term projects from Short term resources, and due to projects stuck in between and going into litigations, it fell short of cash and started defaulting on its obligations. Even due to delays in construction projects, delay in land acquisitions, and approvals, costs escalated. Thus, the rating agencies downgraded the ratings of their short-term and long-term borrowing programs.

The Chairman of IL&FS Group & his team of other directors & senior employees indulged in fraudulent Accounting & Business practices like the evergreening of loans to hide the real financial situation. Auditors suppress information on bad loans and help inflate profits to present a sense of stability. The debt of the group rose to 94,000 crores.

IL&FS had created a trust known as the Employee Welfare Trust, which was used as an instrument to enrich its directors at the cost of the company. The trust was used to carry out fraud on IL&FS ad its group companies. The trust owned 12% of IL&FS Limited. The Chairman and certain other senior IL&FS personnel were major beneficiaries of the Trust.

The following can be a list of fraud taking place in the group:

a) Indiscriminate sanctioning of loans

b) Diverting of funds

c) Flouting of RBI norms

d) Fraudulent transactions to certain accounts

e) Showing inflated numbers of subsidiaries

f) Conflict of interest and concentration of power in the hands of few.

g) IL&FS was window dressing its financial statements by hiding severe mismatch between its cash flows and payment obligations.

h) It was also hiding a total lack of liquidity and glaring adverse financial ratios

i) Auditors also failed to report on the same

Unfolding Of Fraud

The problems came to light in July 2018 when two of IL&FS's subsidiaries failed to pay back loans and inter-corporate deposits to certain banks and lenders. By September, reports were emerging that IL&FS was struggling to repay amounts in excess of Rs. 1,000 crores to SIDBI.

The First Investigation Report (FIR) was filed by 63 Moons to recover its Rs 200 crore investment in NCDs; it stated that in or around 2018, IL&FS group defaulted on their financial debt/obligations and has been defaulting since then. This busted the activities of IL&FS Group and its key managerial persons. The company itself had admitted the massive liability of Rs 91,000 crore towards various investors and creditors.

Further, the RBI was forced to take action when it became known that IL&FS's NBFC arm, Il&FS Financial Services Limited (IFIN), had been defaulting on commercial paper payments also. During the month of September alone, IL&FS had defaulted on multiple loan payments.

Leading Chartered Accountant firm was appointed as the forensic auditor; it reported circular transactions to fool auditors, regulators, and rating agencies. The entire group was in deep financial trouble since FY 2012-13 but was able to hide its losses through dubious financial transactions till September 2018, i.e., defaulted on a loan of Rs. 1,000 crores to SIDBI.

The group hid losses by moving funds among the 347 of its group companies (some of which were created on the same day).

The Key managerial Personnel took undue advantage of their position and diverted funds from its group companies.

Consequences

The Chairman was the prime accused, as he was the key decision-maker in the IL&FS group. The Chairman, former MD, Vice President, and Director of ITNL were also arrested.

Charges of cheating and alleged criminal conspiracy had been filed against 30 individuals, including the above management personnel and two auditors.

Relevant Sections of the Indian Penal Code (IPC) Involved

Section 420 (Cheating), 120B (Criminal Conspiracy).

References

www.economictimes.indiatimes.com

www.business-standard.com

www.zeenews.india.com

Case Study 24: Fraud Through Journal Entries

Modus Operandi: Manipulation of revenue and expenses

Profit & Loss Account items involved: Revenue (defer the revenue), Closing Stock (Write off inventory), Expenses (Book premature expenses) & after acquisition, reversal of these and to show a very high profit after acquisition.

Balance Sheet items involved: Investment in Subsidiaries

Company Involved: Shiningstar (names changed)

Introduction

George was the CEO of Shiningstar after the demise of his father. He was obsessed with exceeding his father's accomplishments. George, soon after becoming CEO, took Shiningstar public and much to his dismay, found that the stock market brutally punished those who did not meet earnings expectations. Mohit, an external auditor of Shiningstar, was soon appointed as the CFO of the company to support such aggressive acquisitions.

Fraud

Strategy used to mislead investors:

a) The CFO and CEO used a simple tactic to achieve the expected earnings. Mohit drastically cut costs.

b) They followed a strategy to aggressively acquire as many companies as possible so that their earnings would form a part of the consolidated financials.

c) In each new acquisition, Mohit led a team of accountants and auditors from his old accounting firm for these acquired companies. They also changed the way accounting was handled at these companies without much resistance.

d) Mohit instructed the accounts heads of the acquired companies to either defer the revenue of the company, book premature expenses, or write off inventory valuations during the acquisition period. These entries would be reversed when Shiningstar has acquired the company and therefore presenting that the sudden boom of profits is due to the acquisition by Shiningstar.

Unfolding Of Fraud

A whistle-blower who emerged from one of the companies acquired by Shiningstar revealed the fraud. When the press got hold of this information, the stock prices crashed as questions of manufactured earnings through improper accounting were raised.

Consequences

The investigations included financial statement analysis and documentation review but progressed to interviews with the witnesses. Many accountants of the acquired companies were part of this investigation which eventually proved that the CFO and the auditors coerced them to pass such entries during the acquisition period. More than INR 800 crores were awarded to the investors in damages.

The CFO and CEO were dismissed from the company and faced actions from the stock exchange and MCA. Eventually, they were convicted of fraud and served prison time for their actions.

Relevant Sections Of The Indian Penal Code (Ipc) Involved

Section 420 (Cheating), 477A (Falsification of Books of Accounts), 120B (Criminal Conspiracy).

Case Study 25: MSTC Gold Fraud

Modus Operandi: Fraud committed by six companies in connivance with Bank officials and MSTC officials – export of gold without Letter of credit and to fake companies in UAE

Profit & Loss Account items involved: Exports to fraudster buyers in UAE

Company Involved: MSTC, Ushma Jewellers & Packing Exports Pvt. Ltd., Space Mercantile Company Pvt. Ltd., K A Malle Pharmaceutical Pvt. Ltd., Joshi Bullion & Gems Jewellery Pvt. Ltd., Bond Gems Pvt. Ltd.

Introduction

MSTC (Metal Scrap Trading Corporation) a public sector undertaking. It helped international commodity traders establish a market and clientele on a long-term basis. MSTC has its corporate office in Kolkata and is a trading corporation involved in imports & exports and is a nominated agency for Gold Exports. The six companies mentioned above were the gold jewelry manufacturers who contacted MSTC to facilitate the export of gold jewelry to UAE in the year 2008-09.

Fraud

MSTC had targeted the export of gold to Rs. 1,000 crores for the year 2008-09. These six companies approached MSTC for helping them in the export of gold jewelry on payment of fees. The importers in UAE were ready, according to them. Once the shipment was ready and foreign buyers gave the nod for payment, MSTC should pay the domestic companies.

Three four consignments went well, payments were received on time, and the parties were genuine. Initially, the credit period was 30 days which was increased to 60 days, 90 days, 120 days, and ultimately 170 days.

It happened in one of the consignments that the accused exported jewelry worth Rs. 600 crores to various buyers in the UAE. In lieu of this export, MSTC gave advances worth 80 percent of the value of the invoice, viz Rs 480 crore, to the aforesaid Associate Suppliers through RTGS in their nominated bank accounts.

The gold was supposed to be exported to Export Credit Guarantee Corporation (ECGC) authorized importers in UAE against the Letter of Credit (LoC), but in this case, there was no letter of credit. The accused conspired to cheat MSTC and allegedly exported gold to their own companies in UAE. The proceeds, which were to be received within 170 days from the date of export, have not been received to date. The exporters, in connivance with the importers, sold the gold in UAE open market fraudulently with a commission of 2 percent and brought back the proceeds of sale to India through Hawala.

Unfolding Of Fraud

On investigation, it was found that the importers in UAE were not authorized importers under MSTC, and also, the importers were the related parties of the exporters. The export proceeds that were supposed to be routed through MSTC to the exporters the money were allegedly brought in through Hawala, which was routed through Pen Urban Co-operative Bank, whose chairman was the ex-director of Space Mercantile Company Pvt. Ltd., one of the accused companies.

MSTC was unable to recover Rs 480 crore, which led to the loss of Rs 480 crore to the Government of India. It also came out that the six exporters had submitted forged documents, and the three MSTC officials took undue advantage of their official positions as public servants and allegedly accepted the said forged and fake documents and released 80 percent of the export value to them.

Consequences

CBI arrested officials of Pen Urban Co-operative Bank, Some officials of MSTC, and directors of six accused companies, consignees in UAE in 2012.

Relevant Sections Of The Indian Penal Code (IPC) Involved

Section 420 (Cheating MSTC by submitting fake documents), 468 (Forgery for the purpose of cheating), 471 (Use of Forged documents as genuine), 168 (Criminal misconduct by public servant), 120B (Criminal Conspiracy).

References

www.economictimes.indiatimes.com

www.business-standard.com

www.indianexpress.com

Case Study 26: Housing Cheating

Modus Operandi: Cheating by raising loan on property of someone and not using the funds for the purpose it was borrowed

Balance Sheet items involved: Loans to associate companies & Debentures

Company Involved: Matru Habitat Pvt. Ltd. (Names changed)

Introduction

Matru Habitat Pvt. Ltd. (MHPL) is a builder and developer company in Mumbai. Rahul Developers owns land at Virar, which was a big parcel of land occupied by the slum dwellers. Rahul Developers entered into JDA with MHPL in January 2016.

MHPL promised to vacate the slum dwellers and develop the plot by constructing residential and commercial buildings. The consideration in JDA was Rs. Fifty crores to be paid to owners, giving 20 percent share in the constructed property and also paying rent to the slum dwellers (as compensation for their alternate accommodation).

Fraud

Within one month of entering into JDA, MHPL entered into an Indenture of Mortgage with Infra Funds Pvt. Ltd. for the issue of debentures for Rs. 100 crores mortgaging the Virar property of Rahul Developers. MHPL took consent from Rahul Developers only after signing the Indenture of Mortgage. Only after that, they started paying the JDA consideration to Rahul Developers.

MHPL only paid Rs. 20 crores to Rahul developers instead of Rs. 50 crores. After which, they stopped paying. MHPL did not do anything to develop the property, and in fact, after three years, it entered into another Indenture of Mortgage with Infra Funds Pvt. Ltd. for the issue of another set of debentures for Rs. 80 crores without the knowledge of Rahul Developers.

Unfolding Of Fraud

After sending a number of reminders to MHPL, Rahul Developers did not get a satisfactory reply; later, MHPL started not answering the calls from Rahul Developers and started ignoring their communication.

Thus, Rahul Developers filed a complaint with EOW, and on the investigation, the money trail showed that MHPL had diverted the borrowed funds to its associates immediately upon receipt of funds through the issue of debentures. Out of Rs. 150 crores, almost Rs. 90 crores were diverted to its associate companies and to Director's personal accounts.

Consequences

An FIR was filed against Matru Habitat Pvt. Ltd., holding it guilty of Cheating, Criminal conspiracy, and criminal breach of trust.

Relevant Sections Of The Indian Penal Code (IPC) Involved

Section 420 (Cheating), 406 (Criminal breach of trust), 120B (Criminal Conspiracy).

Case Study 27: Road To Cheating

Modus Operandi: Luring the contractor for more work and then paying less than agreed and diverting the funds to domestic and foreign subsidiaries

Profit & Loss Account items involved: Expense (Royalty expense was charged higher by cheating the contractor) & Loans to subsidiary and associate companies and thus diverting the money for purposes other than that for which it was received.

Company Involved: Steve Engineering & Construction Co. Ltd. (Names changed)

Introduction

Steve Engineering & Construction Co. Ltd. (SECCL) was a company taking government the infrastructure contracts. SECCL was appointed for one of such road construction contracts by the Government of Gujrat in September 2010.

Due to overburdened work, it outsourced the contract to Y Engineers on the basis of a 4% royalty on payments received from the government, and they entered into an agreement for the same, contract value being Rs. 300 crores.

Fraud

Upto the first four bills, everything went well. Afterward, SECCL started deducting 6% royalty instead of 4% without communicating the same to Y Engineers.

The contract was completed by May 2016, but SECCL did not pay the royalty difference of 2% and also the retention money, which was received on completion of the contract from the government. This amounted to Rs. 35 crores.

By this time, Y Engineers had entered into 2nd contract with SECCL for Rs. 100 crores contract price. In this 2nd contract, the royalty was decided to be 5%, but as in the first case, SECCL started deducting 7% as royalty on all the running bills.

Somewhere in October 2017, when the contract was 80% completed, Y Engineers' work was stopped, and SECCL hired another contractor APCL. But this time, all men and machinery of Y Engineers were used at the construction site. Thus, after a lot of communication, SECCL and Y Engineers again entered into another contract to pay the outstanding of 2nd contract, Rs. 20 crores, and hire charges of the machinery owned by Y Engineers.

SECCL did not pay a single rupee after entering into the 2nd contract. All the outstanding were written in the new agreement item-wise. But still, SECCL did not pay anything.

Unfolding Of Fraud

After being irritated with continuous follow-ups, Y Engineers filed a complaint against SECCL in EOW in 2021 for a total fraud of Rs. 55 crores (principal amount). Later forensic auditors were appointed, and it was found out that SECCL had diverted the funds to its 38 subsidiaries and associate companies in India and abroad.

Consequences

A First Information Report (FIR) was filed against the Company and its Directors (including past directors) under cheating, criminal conspiracy, and criminal breach of trust.

Relevant Sections Of The Indian Penal Code (IPC) Involved

Section 420 (Cheating), 406 (Criminal Breach of Trust of the Contractor), 120B (Criminal Conspiracy).

Case Study 28: Cheating On Issue Of Shares

Modus Operandi: Taking money against the issue of shares but utilizing the money for buying personal investments

Balance Sheet items involved: Share Investments (in the books of individuals), Loans from Individuals/Directors & Share Capital (in the books of company)

Company Involved: MGM Finance Ltd. (Names Changed)

Introduction

Mr. Ram and Mr. Shyam were in stock broking business in Chennai. One of the old clients approached the duo with an offer to invest in his company for Rs. 30 crores for a 40% stake. They sent the calculations via email through a chartered accountant known to Mr. Ram and Mr. Shyam. After negotiations, the amount was settled at Rs. 26 crores which was agreed between all the parties.

Fraud

Mr. Ram and Mr. Shyam were made the directors of the company and started investing in tranches. They were given 15,00,000 shares in the company. Their investment was shown as a loan from directors for approx. 20 months.

After this, they were approached by the main promoter Mr. Raju who asked them to take back the investment and, as the company, would come out with a rights issue worth INR 40 crore. Mr. Raju and his family members will give the shares out of their own investment in lieu of the amount which will be paid by Mr. Ram and Mr. Shaym to Mr. Raju and his family members in their personal accounts.

A Memorandum of Understanding was made to the effect, which stated clearly that Mr. Raju would make a new company, where his shares would be transferred, and after three months, Mr. Ram and Mr. Shyam will become the directors and shareholders of the new company.

Unfolding Of Fraud

Even after continuous reminders and meetings, Mr. Raju and his family did not perform any of the promises made in the MoU. Thus, Mr. Ram and Shyam filed a complaint.

On investigation, it was found that Mr. Raju had received the rights issue of the company MGM Finance Ltd. and later lending division of MGM Finance was sold to one of the well-known Super Group's companies for which Mr. Raju and his family received shares of Super Group's company worth approx. INR 55 crores (as shares to existing shareholders of MGM were given).

Thus, Mr. Ram and Mr. Shyam made a loss on this part also. Their investment was never paid back, and also their right to the new company's shares was also given.

Consequences

An FIR was filed against Mr. Raju and his family members for cheating Mr. Ram and Mr. Shyam.

Relevant Sections Of The Indian Penal Code (Ipc) Involved

Section 420 (Cheating), Section 403 (Criminal misappropriation of property), Section 406 (Criminal breach of trust), Section 34 (Common intention), Section 120B (Criminal Conspiracy).

Case Study 29: Everything For Family

Modus Operandi: Understating Income, recording income directly in personal account and Inflating Expenditure for siphoning off money of the employer

Profit and Loss Account items involved: Income, Expense

Balance Sheet items involved: Savings account of customer (liability)

Company Involved: Accounts department employee of Dhanwan Bank (names changed)

Introduction

Eknath Mane came from a poor family in a rural area. His accounting degree was a passport to his success. His work ethic was incomparable, and soon he became a role model for what a Dhanwan Bank employee should be. His interest in accounting and clearing operations of the bank gained him the trust and confidence of his supervisors, accounting personnel, and bank tellers. He pushed himself by working for almost 12 hours a day. He had a good reputation and often sent his hard-earned money to his sibling for further education. No one seemed to realize that Eknath's habit of helping his family had become too expensive for him to maintain.

Fraud

Eknath found bookkeeping as routine work that lacked any challenge. He mastered the accounting entries in the branch operations, including check clearing and settlement entries. As a result, the branch accountant entrusted him with the task of posting these entries in the daily financial statement without reviewing the accuracy of these entries.

At first, he learned these entries just out of curiosity, but he quickly spotted a weakness in the system- the branch's income and sundry debit accounts. This Sundry debit account was being used to temporarily post-nominal charges and expenses, which were reversed the following day in the real account. The charges were so small that nobody took notice of it except Eknath, who would do just about anything to help his family back home.

Eknath opened a savings account at the branch he worked. He made various cheque deposits in this account that were drawn from different banks in the area. He presented the deposit slip without the actual corresponding cheque. When the teller asked for cheques, he informed them that they had already been included in outward clearing cheques. the processing tellers had accepted his word and made credit entries to his saving account.

Being in charge of the clearing statements and the daily statement, Eknath manipulated the corresponding accounting entry on the amount credited by the teller to his saving account. To ensure that the amounts credited in his savings account were tallied, he used the following accounting entries:

a) debiting the income account of the branch,

b) under posting the branch's daily income on service charges or fees,

c) debiting sundries debit account.

To avoid an audit trail, he altered the amount posted in the entries under sundry debt, income, savings, and deposit accounts. He then withdrew each fictitious check deposited to his account. This scam went undetected for over seven years. During this time, he was able to deposit approximately 1400 fictitious cheques totaling Rs. 80 lakhs. Thus, he inflated expenditures, understated the income, and siphoned off the bank's funds by manipulating the bank documents.

Unfolding of Fraud

An anonymous caller called the special audit department of Dhanwan Bank, stating that the charges on cleared checks looked suspicious and manipulated and that income looked posted without any supporting documents in the branch where Eknath worked.

As soon as the audit staff reached to the branch, Eknath suddenly filed an emergency leave request and did not return. The audit team was able to intercept a cheque deposit slip for Eknath's saving account. The processing teller had credited Eknath's account without the accompanying cheque. On further questioning, the teller said that it was a regular practice to accept deposits from Eknath without an actual cheque because he assured everyone that the cheque was already included in the outward clearing check items.

The audit team had difficulty retrieving the source documents, Such as statements of accounts, clearing proof sheets, and tellers' journals to establish an audit trail and evidence. It was a painstaking effort on their part to reconstruct all the accounting entries and link together the manipulated accounts. It was difficult to prove Eknath's manipulation of income and sundry accounts due to a lack of direct links to the perpetrator, and the courts considered those entries as circumstantial evidence.

Consequences

Dhanwan Bank terminated Eknath. He also was sentenced to a five-year jail term.

Furthermore, Dhanwan Bank suspended and terminated the tellers who processed Eknath's false deposits, the branch accountant, supervising bookkeeper, the branch operating officer, and the branch manager, although there seemed to be severe sanctions, including suspension and termination.

Relevant Section Of Indian Penal Code (IPC) Involved

Section 420 (Cheating by siphoning off employer's funds), 410 (Possessing Stolen Property of the Company), 406 (Criminal Breach of Trust of Company Management), 477A (Falsification of Accounts), 120B (Criminal Conspiracy).

Case Study 30: VIVO foreign Companies Case

Modus Operandi: Diversion of funds to foreign companies to avoid taxes in India

Profit & Loss Account items involved: Expenses (false expenses to avoid tax payments in India)

Balance Sheet items involved: Creditors (False/excessive creditors for expenses)

False address of promoters in incorporation documents

Company Involved: Vivo Mobile India Ltd.

Introduction

Vivo Mobile India Ltd. is the Indian branch of Chinese mobile manufacturer BBK Electronics. It is one of the biggest smartphone manufacturers in India.

Fraud

Vivo Mobiles India Pvt Ltd was incorporated on August 1, 2014, as a subsidiary of Multi Accord Ltd, a Hong Kong-based company, and was registered at ROC Delhi. GPICPL (Grand Prospect International Communication Pvt. Ltd.) was registered on December 3, 2014, at ROC Shimla, with registered addresses of Solan, Himachal Pradesh, and Gandhinagar, Jammu.

GPICPL was incorporated by Zhengshen Ou, Bin Lou, and Zhang Jie with the help of a chartered accountant. The Chinese counterparts left India by 2021.

ED's investigation revealed that the same director of GPICPL was also an ex-director of Vivo. He had incorporated multiple companies across the country spread across various states, a total of 18 companies around the same time, just after the incorporation of Vivo in the year 2014-15.

Unfolding Of Fraud

ED's investigations were based on the Delhi Police FIR against GPICPL, where its shareholders had been found to forged identification documents and falsified addresses at the time of incorporation. The allegations were found to be true as the investigation revealed that the addresses mentioned by the directors of GPICPL did not belong to them, but in fact, it was a government building and the house of a senior bureaucrat.

Investigations revealed that nearly half the company's profits— amounting to Rs 62,476 crore — had been remitted out of the country and primarily to China. It also has 23 associated companies. These remittances were made in order to disclose huge losses in Indian incorporated companies to avoid payment of taxes in India.

Consequences

The ED carried out searches under PMLA (Prevention of Money Laundering Act) at 48 locations and has blocked 119 bank accounts linked to Vivo's India business which were holding Rs 465 crore, Rs 73 lakh cash, and 2 kg gold bars, as part of a probe into alleged money laundering by the company.

Relevant Section Of Indian Penal Code (IPC) Involved

Section 420 (Cheating the promoter directors), 477A (Falsification of Accounts), 120B (Criminal Conspiracy), 403 (Dishonest misappropriation of property)

References

www.timesofindia.indiatimes.com

www.business-standard.com

www.thehindu.com

Case Study 31: Embezzlement from AIIMS

Modus Operandi: Preparing fake purchase documents and siphoning off money from the company

Profit & Loss Account items involved: Purchases (fake purchase documents), Stock (No stock delivered physically whereas books showed purchases of stock)

Balance Sheet items involved: Stock (No stock delivered physically, whereas books showed purchases of stock) and Payment to Vendor without receipt of goods

Company Involved: Sneh Enterprise and Two Staff Members of AIIMS, Delhi

Introduction

All India Institute of Medical Sciences (AIIMS) is globally renowned and recognized for its technology-driven approach. This makes AIIMS the dream college for all medical aspirants in the country.

Fraud

Bijender Kumar was a storekeeper at AIIMS. He prepared forged purchase proforma, supply orders, and inspection notes and secured the release of payments in favor of Sneh Enterprises. Naveen Kumar was a contractual employee and was posted as Programme Assistant in the office of Dr. Atul Kumar, Ex-Chief Dr Rajender Prasad Eye Center, AIIMS.

Indents for the goods were issued through the official ID of the contracted employee, and the same was also verified by him. Thus, Bills were raised by the Storekeeper and got approved himself.

After getting these bills of 'sham deliveries' sanctioned, the cheated amount used to be transferred to the account of the firm, namely Sneh Enterprises. The firm's account statement confirmed the receipt of payments.

Unfolding Of Fraud

Medical Superintendent at Rajender Prasad Eye Centre, AIIMS, Delhi, had lodged a complaint regarding embezzlement of government funds to the tune of Rs 5 crore (raised to Rs 13.85 crore during the investigation) on account of purchase of linen items. The items were never supplied actually, but payment was released to the supplier firm Sneh Enterprises.

Investigation of the e-way bills revealed that vehicles shown as used for delivery of those goods to AIIMS never delivered the same at AIIMS Delhi on any of the dates mentioned on the e-way bills. Scrutiny of GPS logs of the vehicles appearing on the e-way bills showed their locations out of Delhi. On calling the record from Sneh Enterprises, it submitted only invoices and delivery challans. The Goods receipt was not found in the general stores also.

Consequences

The proprietor of Sneh Enterprises, was arrested.

The storekeeper and the contractual staff, were arrested by the Economic Offence Wing (EOW) of Delhi Police for embezzling government funds to the tune of Rs 13.80 crore.

Relevant Section Of Indian Penal Code (Ipc) Involved

Section 420 (Cheating), 409 (Criminal breach of trust by public servant), 467 (Forgery of valuable security), 468 (Forgery for the purpose of cheating), 471 (Using as genuine a forged document or electronic record), 120B (Criminal Conspiracy).

References

www.timesofindia.indiatimes.com

www.economictimes.com

www.thehindu.com

Case Study 32: Fashionable Way To Cheat

Modus Operandi: Sale of shares of fake company

Balance sheet item involved: Investments (investment in fake Company)

Company Involved: Fresh Fashions India Ltd. (name changed)

Introduction

Sanjay kumar a chartered accountant was having a company by name 'Fresh Fashions India Ltd.' Earlier it was a private limited company, and then it was converted into public limited company.

The company was doing excellent business. It was earning good profits and was regularly paying dividends to shareholders. The informant was told that their company was to start a chain of shops in the entire country and had planned to open 70 shops.

Fraud

In 2017, Mr. Nirmal, a businessman from Mumbai, was introduced to Mr. Sanjay by Mr. Pawan at a wedding at Kolkata. Mr. Pawan said that Mr. Sanjay had some shares of his company for sale and he was ready to sell at lesser than the market price as between Oct 2017 till Sept 2018, Mr. Nirmal purchased 1,37,000 shares for Rs. 34.12 crores in tranches. He received the share certificates of Fresh Fashions India Ltd. in the name of his company.

In September 2018, Mr. Nirmal received an email that he was appointed as the Director of Fresh Fashions India Ltd. in its Annual General Meeting.

Unfolding Of Fraud

Mr. Nirmal kept on asking about the details of the company. Later on, inquiry he found that no such company was in existence. Another company named; Fresh Fashions (India) Pvt. Ltd. was registered with ROC Chennai. But Mr. Sanjay was not its chairman, nor was Mr. Nirmal, a director.

On constant pressure, Mr. Sanjay paid Rs. 19.50 crores to Mr. Nirmal, but still Rs. 14.62 crores was receivable. Thus, an MoU was made in which Mr. Sanjay promised to give two flats in Kolkata to Nirmal's company. But subsequently, it was found that a similar MOU was also made with Pawan Jain, and Mr. Pawan and he had lodged FIR for the same.

Consequences

Based on the complaint from Mr. Nirmal, FIR was lodged. In September 2020, Mr. Sanjay was arrested.

Later it was found that two more people were duped by him for Rs 15 crore and Rs. 5 crore.

Relevant Sections Of The Indian Penal Code (Ipc) Involved

Section 420 (Cheating), 463 (Forgery), 406 (Criminal breach of trust), 120B (Criminal Conspiracy).

References

www.economictimes.indiatimes.com

www.timesofindia.indiatimes.com

www.indiakanoon.org

Case Study 33: Theft Of Statutory Fund

Modus Operandi: Siphoning off employer's funds and using it for personal purposes

Balance Sheet items involved: Payment of Taxes and stamp duty charges on behalf of clients and Bank (all payments done through bank account into his personal account – as he was authorized to approve payments upto Rs. 1.50 lakhs

Company Involved: ABC Associates (law firm – names changed)

Introduction

ABC Associates is a law firm in Delhi. The firm's General Manager (Finance) was Mr. Kant, a qualified CA (Charted Accountant) with a monthly salary of Rs 4.5 lakhs.

Fraud

The General Manager made several bogus/forged entries in the firms' accounting software, and these entries/transactions were made on the false pretext of payments for taxes or stamp duty of certain clients.

He indulged in the creation of bogus entries in the accounting software of the employer either through himself or through his subordinates. He was the person being competent to authorize the approvals for the payments up to Rs 1.5 lakhs. He approved more than 2300 entries in one and a half years.

Through such transactions, he diverted the funds of the firm into the personal bank. account. He uploaded the requests on the online banking portal of his firm and approved the payments in the software of the firm.

Unfolding Of Fraud

A complaint was made by partners of ABC Associates, stating therein that the alleged Mr. Kant, General Manager (Finance) in their firm and he had diverted the funds of the firm in his personal account and misappropriated the same.

During the Covid pandemic, Mr. Kant, the accused, diverted Rs 27.28 Crore in his personal bank account and misappropriated these funds. It was also revealed that the accused had invested this money in the share market and booked losses in options trading.

Consequences

EOW Delhi arrested The General Manager for diverting Rs 27.3 crore of his employer's money.

Relevant Section Of Indian Penal Code (IPC) Involved

Section 420 (Cheating the firm and partners by misappropriating the firm's funds), 405 (Criminal Breach of Trust), 477A (Falsification of Accounts), 120B (Criminal Conspiracy).

References

www.policeworld.businessworld.in

www.timesofindia.indiatimes.com

www.lokmttimes.com

Case Study 34: Quick Getaway

Modus Operandi: Making forged documents and diverting the money to foreign Chinese-controlled shell companies

Profit & Loss Account item involved: Expenses (forged expense), Forged documents for expenses and remittances to shell companies in Hongkong, SAR, China

Company Involved: Chinese Controlled Companies

Introduction

ED has been conducting Money Laundering investigation against a number of Chinese controlled companies namely M/s Linkyun Technology Private Limited and M/s Dokypay Technology Private Limited, who had cheated lakhs of gullible online users through illegal Gaming, Dating & Streaming Applications; and collected thousands of crore via online Payment gateways and then laundered the money using various modus operandi including hawala payments to Hair merchants, purchase of crypto-currency, illegal remittances to Singapore, etc.

Fraud

Some persons laundered Rs 1146 Crore to Hong Kong by sending Foreign Outward Remittances from select Bank branches of State Bank of India and State Bank of Mauritius at Mumbai by using forged Air Way Bills (AWBs) of Reputed companies in the name of Freight Forwarding Services and fabricated invoices in the name of import of Cloud CCTV Storage Rental services.

An Indian Chartered Accountant, without doing any due diligence and without verification of genuineness of import documents, had issued 621 bogus Form 15CB certificates and blindly signed the balance sheets of Shell companies/firms which enabled them to launder the proceeds of crime, to Hong Kong, SAR, China. He is more responsible as he is a professional, he failed in his statutory duty and assisted the accused persons and charged Rs 1500 per bogus certificate and thus got involved in the offense of money laundering for personal gain. The proprietors of the shell firms are absconding.

An entry operator was using the shell companies to launder the money.

Unfolding Of Fraud

During the course of the ongoing fund trail investigation, ED came across the new modus operandi of using fake Air Way Bills and fake Cloud Rental Bills to send bogus foreign outward remittances from multiple Bank accounts. On the basis of a fund trail investigation of suspect Bank Accounts and analysis of IT and GST returns, ED traced the entry operator. It was found that he was the entry operator using the shell companies to launder the money. These Shell companies received laundered money partly from Chinese companies and partly from other suspicious unconnected entities to the tune of Rs 1146 Crore; in turn, this laundered money was sent out as foreign outward remittances based on fake certificates/documents.

Consequences

The Chartered accountant as well as the Entry Operator were arrested by ED, and further investigation into the mastermind is still on. Proprietors of shell firms are absconding.

Relevant Sections Of The Indian Penal Code (IPC) Involved

Section 420 (Cheating), 465 (Forgery), 405 (Criminal Breach of Trust), 477A (Falsification of Accounts), 120B (Criminal Conspiracy).

References

www.timesofindia.indiatimes.com

www.ndtv.com

www.economictimes.com

Case Study 35: Paper Turnover Companies

Modus Operandi: Making paper turnover within related companies to avail bank loans at different levels and locations with an intent to siphon out the entire loan for making personal properties instead of utilizing the same for the purpose of business.

Profit & Loss Account items involved: Sales (Showing fake sales to shell companies), Closing Stock (Overvalued), Purchases (Showing fake purchases from shell companies), and Business was shown as very high so as to avail bank loans.

Balance Sheet items involved: Loans to shell companies and then using the money for buying personal properties and Loans from Banks.

Company Involved: Shaktibhog Foods Ltd.

Introduction

Shaktibhog Foods Ltd. is a 24-year-old company, which is into manufacturing and selling wheat, flour, rice, biscuits, cookies, etc., had organically grown as it ventured into food-related diversification over a decade with a turnover growth of Rs 1,411 crore in 2008 to Rs 6,000 crore in 2014. The growth came to an abrupt halt in 2015, with the account turning into a Non-Performing Asset (NPA).

Fraud

Two outside parties also assisted the company and the directors in generating loans, layering, and siphoning off its loan funds through shell companies under them. Thus, they provided fake sale-purchase invoices from dummy entities without allegedly having any genuine business transactions. There was round-tripping of funds and suspicious payments made by the company and also manipulation of account books. The loan was taken to the tune of Rs. 3,269 crores from a consortium of 10 banks led by the State Bank of India.

Unfolding Of Fraud

a. According to the SBI complaint, the directors allegedly falsified accounts and forged documents to siphon off public funds.

b. The forensic audit done by the bankers pointed out that the company, in its account books for the financial year 2015-16, showed that its inventory worth over Rs 3,000 crore got damaged due to pests and was sold at substantially low prices.

c. This was contradictory to the stock and receivable audit report, which showed that the company had a stock of over Rs 3,500 crore in September 2015, its warehouses were fully stocked, and none of the inventory was obsolete or slow moving.

d. The report also said the company had an insurance policy for protection against fire, earthquake, and other perils but no claims were made about stock getting damaged because of pests.

e. The accounts also did not show any receivables owing to a sale of damaged stocks at low prices.

Consequences

a. The ED had initiated a money laundering investigation on the basis of an FIR registered by the Central Bureau of Investigation (CBI) against Shakti Bhog Foods Limited and others for criminal conspiracy, cheating, and criminal misconduct resulting in bank fraud of Rs 3269.42 crore.

b. According to the officials, these arrests were preceded by searches carried out by the ED on September 17, 2021, at 13 premises in Delhi and Uttar Pradesh.

c. All accused, including the co-conspirators, directors, Chartered Accountant of the company, were arrested.

Relevant Sections Of The Indian Penal Code (Ipc) Involved

Section 420 (Cheating), 120B (Criminal Conspiracy).

References

www.economictimes.indiatimes.com

www.business-standard.com

Case Study 36: Merry Go Round

Modus Operandi: Creating group companies and then diverting the funds for personal gain, making fake debtors and then writing off the same.

Profit & Loss Account items involved: Commission given, Bad Debts written off, rent paid, and Discount received

Balance Sheet items involved: Advance to Debtors and Debtors outstanding for a long time

Company Involved: Raja Textiles Pvt. Ltd. (Names changed)

Introduction

Raja Textiles Pvt. Ltd. (RTPL) is a company incorporated in 2014 doing the business of trading in cotton yarn. It has four directors, and all four directors are the shareholders. The directors of the company are Mr. Anil Sharma and Mr. Sunil Sharma (Sharma Group) and Mr. Mohan Gupta and Mr. Sohan Gupta (Gupta Group). Gupta Group was entrusted with the responsibility of day-to-day management of the company, and all cheque signing authority was also in the hands of Gupta Group.

Fraud

Gupta group having all the authority of day-to-day management and signing authority for banks, has committed the following frauds to the tune of Rs. 28.20 crores:

a) Debtors outstanding for Rs. 12.22 crores from 7 parties since a long time. On investigation, it was found that out of seven parties, two parties were having the Gupta group as directors, thus they were related parties. From the remaining five parties, the consideration was received by related parties of the Gupta group instead of RTPL.

b) Commission of Rs. 0.55 crores was paid to the related parties of the Gupta group for which no contract was signed and has no supporting documents.

c) Commission of Rs. 3.15 crores was paid to parties without any justification and documentation in the last five years for which the Gupta group has taken cash components from such parties.

d) Advances to be given to parties to the tune of Rs. 3.09 crores which were further diverted to one of the companies of relatives of the Gupta group and later it was transferred to their personal accounts.

e) Bad Debts are written off to the tune of Rs. 4.17 crores for which no effort was made to recover the money, and it was later discovered that there was collusion between one of the parties and the Gupta group.

f) Cash withdrawn in last five years amounting to Rs. 1.21 crores by Gupta group without any valid explanation for the same.

g) There was a fictitious rent payment of Rs. 0.05 crores to the wife of Mr. Sohan Gupta for which the company has never used any premises or any other asset and also there was no agreement for the same.

h) It was observed that the Gupta group has accommodated one of their suppliers to the extent of Rs 3.76 crores by foregoing the discounts that RTPL should have received as per the terms and conditions of purchase.

Unfolding Of Fraud

During the year 2021-22, certain transactions were questionable in the eyes of the Sharma group, and prima facie, it looked like a fraud. Thus, the Sharma group took the help of a Forensic auditor. It was also noticed that the other companies in which the Gupta group were directors were defrauded by public sector banks by siphoning off funds to their related companies and then the loans became NPA. Thus, a fraud of Rs. 28.20 was committed by the Gupta group.

Consequences

On complaint to EOW by Sharma group, PE was registered. But later there was a settlement between the parties and the matter was resolved.

Relevant Sections Of The Indian Penal Code (IPC) Involved

Section 420 (Cheating the other directors and shareholders), 406 (Criminal Breach of Trust), 477A (Falsification of Accounts), 120B (Criminal Conspiracy).

Case Study 37: Hand In Glove With Bank Officials

Modus Operandi: Taking loan and giving kickback along with siphoning off the loan money

Balance Sheet items involved: Loans to related company of promoter of Yes Bank which was given as kickback of the debenture proceeds, Loans from Bank and Debentures

Company Involved: Deewan Housing Finance Ltd. (DHFL)

Introduction

Deewan Housing Finance Ltd. (DHFL) is a housing loan finance company promoted by two brothers Kapil Wadhwan and Dheeraj Wadhwan. Whereas, Yes Bank is an Indian Bank founded by Rana Kapoor and Ashok Kapoor.

Fraud

Between April 2018 to June 2018, Yes Bank bought short-term Debentures worth Rs. 3,700 crores from DHFL (i.e. DHFL issued debentures to Yes Bank). Thus, an amount of Rs. 3,700 crores was transferred to DHFL.

Out of this amount immediately after the issue of debentures, DHFL gave a loan of Rs. 600 crores to DoIT Urban Ventures Pvt. Ltd. (one of the companies related to the promoter of Yes Bank) by pledging highly overvalued property, the real worth of which is only Rs. 37 crores.

Yes, Bank used money belonging to the public for the purchase of these debentures, which are not yet paid in 2022. Thus, this Rs. 600 crore can be regarded as a kickback for the loan of Rs. 3,700 crore.

Other than the above transaction, Yes Bank had also sanctioned a loan of Rs. 750 crores to the Promoter of DHFL's other company, M/s. Belief Realtors Pvt. Ltd. was given for the development of its Bandra reclamation project (investigations revealed that the entire amount was siphoned off and not used for the purpose for which it was given). The amount was layered through shell companies.

Unfolding Of Fraud

While investing another case against the Founder of Yes Bank, this fraud came to light.

Consequences

All parties involved were arrested for siphoning off Rs. 5,050 crores through suspicious transactions.

Relevant Section Of Indian Penal Code (Ipc) Involved

Section 420 (Cheating), 120B (Criminal Conspiracy), Under PMLA.

References

www.economictimes.indiatimes.com

www.business-standard.com

www.news18.com

Case Study 38: Midas Touch

Modus Operandi: Making of false purchase documents and taking the purchases home for personal purposes, forgery of the signature of colleague

Profit & Loss Account item involved: Purchases (False purchase documents were purchased and gold coins were embezzled for personal use)

Balance Sheet items involved: Creditors remained outstanding for a long time, and thus they complained of not receiving payments

Company Involved: Deputy General Manager of Godrej Consumer Products Ltd.

Introduction

Mr. Ashok (name chaged) was Deputy General Manager (Purchase) for Godrej Consumer Products Ltd. The company generally gave 50 gm gold coins to its retailers and dealers as an incentive. The company generally used to purchase these gold coins from jewelers from Mumbai, Kolkata, etc. and used to pay within 15-20 days.

Fraud

The said Manager was one point of contact with jewelers for the purchase of these gold coins. He misused the position and started buying these gold coins from various jewelers. With the help of his two associates, he sold some of these coins in the market and paid a few jewelers. But later, stopped the payment to them.

He had projected himself as acting on behalf of the company and had forged the signatures of some of the officers of the company, and had also created false purchase orders, emails, etc.

Unfolding Of Fraud

One of the jewelers, Laxmi Dia Jewel, who had supplied 13 gold coins of 50 grams each in December 2008, lodged the complaint with Mumbai EOW against Godrej Consumer Products Ltd. and its employees when it learned that some of the prominent Mumbai jewelers and one from Kolkata also has not been paid. It lodged the complaint for 2.61 crores. Later, Basanti Gold Pvt. Ltd. stated that it had to receive Rs. 8 crores from Godrej.

Consequences

Later, the total fraud came out to be of Rs. 25 crores. Godrej also filed a complaint against the Manager. He and his two associates, were arrested. He had purchased some jewelry and property, which were confiscated.

Relevant Sections Of The Indian Penal Code (IPC) Involved

Section 420 (Cheating), 120B (Criminal Conspiracy).

References

www.economictimes.indiatimes.com

www.livemint.com

www.indiakanoon.org

Case Study 39: HDIL-PMC Scam

Modus Operandi: Taking a loan from the bank and using it for purposes other than for what it is given, siphoning off the money by buying personal property, manipulating bank records

Profit & Loss Account items involved: Payment of routine administrative expenses out of loan borrowed

Balance Sheet items involved: Buying fixed assets and Loans from Banks, paying old loans of group companies

Company Involved: HDIL & PMC Bank

Introduction

Housing Development & Infrastructure Ltd. (HDIL) is a company incorporated for real estate development in 1996. Mr. Rakesh Wadhwan and Mr. Sarang Wadhwan are the promoter directors of HDIL. Punjab and Maharashtra Co-operative Bank Ltd. is a multistate co-operative bank having branches spread over 10-12 states in India. It is regulated by the Reserve Bank of India. Mr. Waryam Singh was the Chairman of the Bank.

Fraud

HDIL held 44 accounts of their group companies with the bank. From the year 2011, it started defaulting on various loans, but no steps/actions were taken by the bank. In fact, bank officials forged the Advance Master Indent and Off-Site Surveillance (OSS) statements.

They used to create additional fictitious accounts to hide the dues of HDIL. The officials kept on uploading the details such as sanction amount, sanction date, sanction limit, expiry date, security value, etc., of the loans. The number of fake accounts kept on increasing as every year HDIL kept defaulting on loans. At the end of March 2018, there were 21,049 fake accounts.

HDIL kept on taking loans from PMC Bank for the purpose of evergreening the loans taken from other banks and financial institutions. The company took loans amounting to Rs. 6,700 crores from PMC bank.

The loan amounts were used for the evergreening of loans, buying properties, repaying old loans of group companies, paying salaries to employees, etc.

Unfolding Of Fraud

Instead of showing NPA bank officials accommodated the HDIL group. This fraud was unfolded in September 2019 when RBI discovered that there were fictitious loan accounts in the bank to hide more than Rs. 4,355 crores of loans given to HDIL.

Consequences

All related parties i.e. the management of HDIL, Bank Chairman and 20 other officers were also charge-sheeted.

Relevant Sections Of The Indian Penal Code (IPC) Involved

Section 420 (Cheating), 409 (Criminal breach of trust by public servant), 465 (Forgery), 466 (Forgery of record of court or of public register), 471 (Using as genuine a forged document or electronic record), 120B (Criminal Conspiracy).

References

www.economictimes.indiatimes.com

www.business-standard.com

www.livemint.com

Case Study 40: Horizon Is Always Far

Modus Operandi: Using various methods to over-value the business valuation to attract investors.

Profit & Loss Account items involved: Understated Sales and Overstated Expense

Balance Sheet items involved: Understated Debtors, Overstated Liabilities, and understated creditors for goods

Company Involved: Zenith Futures Ltd. (Names changed)

Introduction

Minesh and Mona, a husband and a wife who were the promoters of ZFL and were born in ultra-rich families and were very wealthy. They were the CEO and CFO of the company. Both of them managed the company very well.

Fraud

About 15 years after the ZFL was incorporated, Horizon Ltd., a multinational company was interested in acquiring the company. Horizon acquired ZFL for Rs. 500 crores. Minesh and Mona had committed fraud as follows to increase the valuation of the business (which was revealed by the forensic auditors after five years of the acquisition):

a) Sales entries were not made transaction-wise but were made in batches. There were many credit notes and deleted sales entries offsetting sales. (This was a red flag for auditors)

b) When debtors issued cheques for the transactions (which were either deleted/credit notes were shown), the cheques were deposited in the overseas bank account which was not related to ZFL.

c) A journal entry was passed debiting sales and crediting debtors for Rs. 50 lakhs (was treated as a credit note). Thus, reducing sales and debtors both. Siphoning off money received from these accounts to personal accounts, thus, cash was also shown less.

d) Instead of receiving cash/cheque from debtors, debtors were told to pay Minesh and Mona's personal expenses directly for which credit notes were shown in books.

e) Expenditures were overstated by paying the personal expenses of Minesh and Mona from the business and considering the same as business expenses.

f) Certain staff members were told not to show certain inventory to auditors and change its location and later to sell it in foreign markets and transfer the money to offshore accounts.

Unfolding Of Fraud

After five years of acquisition, it was found that ZFL was not performing as expected. The financial goals were not achievable for ZFL. Thus, forensic auditors were appointed.

Consequences

In this manner when a forensic audit was done for 7 years before the acquisition, the valuation was fraudulently overstated by Rs. 240 crores (almost 50%). The court awarded the damages to Horizon to the extent of Rs. 150 crores.

Relevant Sections Of The Indian Penal Code (Ipc) Involved

Section 420 (Cheating), 406 (Criminal Breach of Trust), 477A (Falsification of Accounts), 120B (Criminal Conspiracy).

Case Study 41: Secret Warehouses

Modus Operandi: Setting up secret warehouses, manipulation of accounts and fictitious/bogus sales

Profit & Loss Account items involved: Inflated Sales and Sales returns not shown

Balance Sheet items involved: Inflated/fake debtors

Company Involved: Reebok India

Introduction

Reebok India is a subsidiary of Reebok International which was acquired by Adidas AG in 2005.

Fraud

The MD, Mr. Shubhinder Singh Prem, and the COO Mr. Vishnu Bhagat, had owned secret warehouses.

The goods were shown as sold to its dealers and distributors but it was only to inflate the sales to meet the target.

The goods returned by dealers and distributors were stored in secret warehouses but were not shown as sales returns, just not to decrease the sales and show the inflated figure of sales.

The sales price was shown higher with a retrospective effect in prices of goods already sold to dealers and distributors.

Some goods which were shown defective worth Rs. 21.5 crores were shown as sold to KK Enterprises which were transferred to the secret warehouses and sold from there to some unauthorized buyers.

Thus, these two officers, set up secret warehouses, manipulated accounts, and were engaged in fictitious sales for several years.

Unfolding Of Fraud

In May 2012 Adidas saw some suspicious transactions and started an investigation. The investigation report was also pointing towards some unauthorized franchise referral program that was run by these two officers and money was collected on the pretext of opening new stores against the instructions from Adidas.

Consequences

The management along with 10 other people, either former employees or associates were arrested for Rs. 870 crore fraud.

Relevant Sections Of The Indian Penal Code (IPC) Involved

Section 420 (Cheating), 120B (Criminal Conspiracy), 477A (Falsification of books of accounts), 463 (Forgery), 471 (Using as genuine a forged document or electronic record).

References

www.livemint.com

www.indiatoday.in

www.thehindubusinessline.com

Case Study 42: Saradha Scam – Ponzi Scheme - MPID Case

Modus Operandi: Ponzi scheme – making vicious circle or a chain to perpetrate fraud by attractive schemes for public

Profit & Loss Account items involved: Interest was paid out of money collected from other investors

Balance Sheet items involved: Funds from public and repayment

Company Involved: Saradha Group of Companies

Introduction

Saradha group of companies was set up by Sudipto Sen. The company has launched collective investment scheme. Saradha Group of companies was a consortium of companies to tap small investors in northeast India by promising very high returns.

Fraud

The group lured the investors through glossy brochures and promising abnormally high returns. An investor could invest from Rs. 100 to any amount. The group collected a huge sum of money through a wide network of agents (almost 2.5 to 3 lakh agents, many of them were investors too) and the consortium of 239 group companies. The group used to pay a very high commission of over 25% to 40% to its agents.

Film stars were endorsing the brand, the brand was also endorsed through popular football clubs, and multi-media outlets were also owned by the group.

The brand was also advertised through sponsorships of cultural events such as Durga Puja, etc. Soon the investors reached 17 lakhs. The group collected almost Rs. 2500 crores in a short span of time.

It was a Ponzi scheme where the investor's principal and interest were repaid from the new investor's investment. A large portion of the group's funds were parked in Dubai, South Africa, and Singapore.

Unfolding Of Fraud

In 2012, SEBI asked the group to stop accepting money from investors and obtain the regulator's permission to run its scheme. In 2013 January, the crisis started in the company for the first time, when its cash inflows were lower than its outflows. By April 1, 2013 agents and investors filed police complaints for non-receipt of the money.

Consequences

In April 2013, all related parties were arrested.

Relevant Sections Of The Indian Penal Code (IPC) Involved

Section 420 (Cheating), 120B (Criminal Conspiracy), 403 (dishonest misappropriation of property), 405 (criminal breach of trust).

References

www.timesofindia.indiatimes.com

www.business-standard.com

www.indiatoday.in

Case Study 43: IMA Scam – Ponzi Scheme - MPID Case

Modus Operandi: Collecting money from people in the name of investing in gold and giving high returns and later duping the investors by not making any repayments.

Balance Sheet items involved: Investments of public money into gold and repayment of the same

Company Involved: I Monetary Advisory

Introduction

Mohammad Mansoor Khan started his advisory I Monetary Advisory (IMA) in 2006 which floated an investment scheme which represented that it was in line with Sharia principles of Islam. He offered very high returns with very low risk.

Fraud

The group raised deposits to the tune of Rs. 4,000 crores from middle-class innocent investors in Bengaluru. He advertised that the investment would be in gold.

He asked Maulvis and Netas to talk about his scheme. He and his employees used to go to Masjid for Namaz in full white pajama-kurta.

Those who become 'partner' by investing were given a copy of the Quran. He donated huge sums to Masjid and Madarsas. Thus, he won the confidence of the people.

Initially, he gave good returns. Slowly returns started decreasing from 9% to 5% and then to 3% and ultimately when it became 1% people started complaining.

In 2019 February, on Eid, he fled from the country. By that time, he had collected deposits of more than 4,000 crores from lakhs of small, innocent investors.

Unfolding of fraud: It was a shock to investors when returns fell and then stopped and during the Eid holiday, he went underground. CBI started investigations.

Consequences

ED arrested him and around 24 other people in connection with the scam.

Relevant Sections Of The Indian Penal Code (IPC) Involved

Section 420 (Cheating), 120B (Criminal Conspiracy), 403 (dishonest misappropriation of property), 405 (criminal breach of trust).

References

www.economictimes.indiatimes.com

www.indianexpress.com

www.thehindu.com

Case Study 44: Parmalat, an old scam-fraud through Domestic and foreign subsidiaries

Modus Operandi: the company incorporated 214 subsidiaries in 48 different countries to siphon off companies fund and then inflated sales and debtors for availing bank loans, showing fictitious bank account and siphoning off company's funds for the purchase of personal assets

Profit & Loss Account items involved: Sales (fake sales/fake double billings/inflated sales to subsidiaries)

Balance Sheet items involved: Fake debtors (inflated debtors – to be shown as collateral for banks), Fake bank account was shown with Euro 4 billion balance, Fake debtors assigned to overseas subsidiaries and Loans from Banks

Company Involved: Parmalat

Introduction

Parmalat is in the business of dairy and food products. It was founded in 1961 as a family-run farm business. It grew into one of the largest dairy and food companies in Italy.

Fraud

The fraud at Parmalat began in 1990 and lasted till 2003. In 2003, Parmalat had 214 subsidiaries in 48 different countries. Parmalat fraud had the following Modus operandi:

a) The revenue was inflated (fake sales). A double billing scheme was adopted to inflate revenue. The amount was billed to even the shipping company (almost 300 employees knew about this).

b) With double billing/fake sales billing, fake debtors/receivables were appearing in Balance Sheet which was used as collateral for taking new loans.

c) Actually, Parmalat started making losses in 1990, but instead of taking corrective measures, the management wanted to hide the losses and, thus, show artificial/fake profits by inflating revenue.

d) Later debtors were assigned to its subsidiary companies and thus, a fictitious cash balance was shown.

e) Even, the debt was shown as equity (as a measure of window dressing) to defraud the investors and lenders.

f) A huge amount of debt was understated (to show a good picture of the affairs of the company)

CEO and other 16 employees misappropriated Euro 1 billion to buy personal assets.

In January 2003 Euro 300 million Eurobond issue was announced and then withdrawn due to which the company's share prices were largely affected.

In December 2003, in spite of having Euro 4 billion in cash and short-term assets, the company had Euro 150 million Eurobond payable, which it failed to pay.

In March 2003, a forged verification letter (with a forged signature of a Bank of America employee) was given to the auditor who thought there was some problem in the company.

Unfolding Of Fraud

In 1997, the auditor of the company noted manipulation in the books amounting to Euro 5 billion, but it was ignored then.

The fraud started unfolding when Parmalat failed to pay Euro 150 million despite having cash and short-term assets of Euro 4 billion on 8th December 2003.

On 9th December 2003, the bond rating was degraded to junk, and the company's stock prices fell by 40%.

On 15th December 2003, CEO stepped down and the board hired a turnaround strategist to resolve the crisis.

On 19th December 2003, the auditor announced that Euro 3.95 billion cash was missing, i.e. an account that was shown in Bank of America does not exist.

Consequences

a) Parmalat's shares were delisted. Later Parmalat was declared insolvent and the CEO was held for fraud.

b) CEO was sentenced to jail for 18 years at the age of 72.

c) Chief Corporate Finance Officer of Bank of America was booked for fraud as he participated in a kickback scheme and received $27 million.

Relevant Section Of Indian Penal Code (Ipc) Involved

Section 420 (Cheating), 406 (Criminal Breach of Trust), 477A (Falsification of Accounts), 463 (Forgery), 409 (Criminal breach of trust by public servant), 120B (Criminal Conspiracy).

References

www.reuters.com

www.ukessays.com

www.forbes.com

Case Study 45: 1mdb Scandal- Scam At Highest Level By Abusing Position

Modus Operandi: Bonds issued by Malaysian Government and then layering the proceeds in shell companies and siphoning off of the same by government officials

Balance Sheet items involved: Loans to shell companies and Government Bonds

Company Involved: 1Malaysia Development Berhad (1MDB)

Introduction

In 2009, 1MDB, a government company was launched by Malaysia to promote foreign investment and partnerships.

Fraud

Government bonds were issued for huge sums and then later the funds were siphoned off and deposited in Swiss, Singapore, and US accounts. Roger Ng (an employee of Goldman Sachs), Tim Leissner (Southeast Asia Chairman of Goldman Sachs and Boss of Roger Ng), and Jho Low (Malaysian Financer) conspired to bribe Goldman officials so that it could arrange USD 6.5 billion in bond offering for 1MDB.

Funds were layered in different entities and individuals and transferred from projects so that a money trail could not be obtained. Goldman Sachs employees was paid a huge commission on these transfers.

All these three-person lifestyles changed. They indulged themselves in huge parties where they invited celebrities, used private jets, etc

The accused transferred funds from former 1MDB unit SRC International to a complex network of shell companies and ultimately to his account.

Unfolding Of Fraud

In 2015, a British Journalist Clare Rewcastle Brown was handling the leaked documents related to the depth of fraud, and thus, the Malaysian Anti-Corruption Agency began investigations and later issued a warrant to arrest all conspirators. Properties worth USD 273 million were confiscated from him.

Consequences

a) All conspirators were arrested.

b) The Malaysian counterpart of this scheme ran out of the country and was declared a fugitive and later, his yacht was found with 1MDB's money in Bali which was seized.

c) Goldman Sachs's Malaysian subsidiary was pleaded guilty.

Relevant Sections Of The Indian Penal Code (IPC) Involved

Section 420 (Cheating), 120B (Criminal Conspiracy), 477A (Falsification of Accounts), 409 (Criminal breach of trust by public servant), 403 (Dishonest misappropriation of property).

References

www.news18.com

www.business-standard.com

www.thehindu.com

Case Study 46: Toshiba Accounting Scandal – Window Dressing Of Accounts

Modus Operandi: Manipulation of accounts by booking future profits, differing expenses and delay in recording purchases

Profit & Loss Account items involved: Sales, purchases, and expenses

Balance Sheet: Reserves and surplus

Company Involved: Toshiba Corporation, Japan

Introduction

Toshiba Corporation was incorporated in 1875 and is one of the pioneers for many innovative products. It has more than 2 lakh employees worldwide.

Fraud

In 2008, the whole world was facing a financial crisis. Toshiba Corporation was also facing a financial crisis in 2008. It was not able to meet its financial targets thus, profitability was affected.

Different business units resorted to different inappropriate accounting techniques to raise the profits:

a) Booking future profits early (next year's profit in this year) – against the principle of conservatism

b) Differing expenditures – recording the expenditure in the future periods

c) Pushing back losses – Losses of the current period to be recorded in the next period

The management knew about these inappropriate accounting practices as everyone wanted to show higher profits. This resulted in an overstatement of profits. This led to a commitment of $ 1.22 billion in accounting fraud. The profits were stated up by three times the actual profits.

Unfolding Of Fraud

The fraud was highlighted by a whistle-blower in early 2015. Investigations revealed that the fraud had been going on for the last seven years with the involvement of senior management. The company's top management had set unrealistic profit targets, which slowly led to the inappropriate accounting practices since failures were not accepted in the company. Thus, this was the only way for the divisional heads to achieve targets and hide the data.

Consequences

In July 2015, the CEO resigned due to a huge accounting fraud. All eight senior officials, including the previous CEI, also resigned. Due to this accounting fraud, the market price of shares of Toshiba declined sharply.

Relevant Sections Of The Indian Penal Code (Ipc) Involved

Section 420 (Cheating), 477A (Falsification of Accounts), 120B (Criminal Conspiracy), 406 (Criminal breach of trust).

References

www.reuters.com

www.businessinsider.com

www.thehindubusinessline.com

Case Study 47: Crazy Eddie – IPO Scandal

Modus Operandi: Cash sales not recorded in books and then introducing cash sales later as preparation for IPO and selling promoter shares once market prices rise.

Profit & Loss Account items involved: Sales, Expenses, discounts, rebates from creditors

Balance Sheet items involved: Debtors and Creditors

Company Involved: Crazy Eddie

Introduction

Crazy Eddie was a family-owned electronics and appliances retail chain stores which was incorporated as a private company in the 1960s. It was run by the Antar Family. It was known for the best price bargains.

Fraud

The fraud was committed in three phases:

a) **Phase I (1969 – 79): Under-Reporting Income**

   i. Selling for cash so that income goes unreported and tax can be avoided.

   ii. Paying employee's salaries in cash so that to avoid payroll taxes (by not entering them in books of accounts)

   iii. Reporting exaggerated insurance claims to increase profits

b) **Phase Ii (1980 – 84): Gradually Reducing Underreporting As Preparing For Ipo**

  i. Stocks were unloaded at inflated prices – to show higher income

  ii. Before the company becomes a public company, growth needs to be shown so that the share prices increase, thus, artificial growth in sales was shown by bringing down the profits a year before the IPO and showing year-on-year growth (whereas actual growth was meager). Management just reduced cash sales and started showing in books.

  iii. As cash sales started reducing, the company could no longer pay employees in cash, which was now to be paid by cheque. Thus, expenses increased. Salary expenses increased drastically, showing a high rise in employee salaries. Salaries increased 3 to 20 times.

  iv. Huge funds were transferred from Israel, and Panama to show it as cash sales, and that way cash was infused into business again

c) **Phase Iii (1984 – 87): After Going Public, Overstating Income So That Insiders Can Sell The Shares At Inflated Prices**

  i. In September 1984 Crazy Eddie came with IPO.

  ii. As the market price increased within 3 years of going public, the Antar family sold off its shares for $ 90 million.

iii. Losses started mounting but to hide the losses, massive inventory was shown, and false incomes like, advertising rebates, and volume discounts were shown.

Unfolding Of Fraud

In 1987 when the company was taken over by the new management due to losses, the fraud started unfolding as inventory shortages were noticed. Thus, investigations started.

Consequences

Both the masterminds from Antar family were sentenced to jail and $ 77 million was fined to them.

Relevant Section Of Indian Penal Code (IPC) Involved

Section 420 (Cheating), 477A (Falsification of accounts), 120B (Criminal Conspiracy), 403 (Dishonest misappropriation of property), 471 (Using as genuine a forged document or electronic record), 406 (Criminal breach of trust), 463 (Forgery).

Case Study 48: NSEL Scam

Modus Operandi: Warehouse receipts not backed by physical inventory (thus companies traded on paper)

Profit & Loss Account items involved: Closing Stock and Purchases

Company Involved: National Spot Exchange Ltd. (NSEL)

Introduction

NSEL was incorporated in 2005 as a company under the Companies Act, 1956 with its registered address in the State of Maharashtra. It was incorporated by MCX and nominees of Financial Technologies India Ltd. (FTIL), now known as 63 Moons Technologies Ltd. It was set up to have a common commodity exchange for Agricultural as well as Industrial goods at the national level. It commenced live trading in 2008. Commodity Exchanges were regulated by Forward Market Commission (FMC) then.

Fraud

a. NSEL was the first electronic commodity exchange for spot delivery of contracts including agricultural goods. Actual time allowed to settle the contract was up to 1+1 days. But the exchange took 25-35 days.

b. Actually, the Exchange was giving long-term loans which were termed as paired forward contracts, which were illegal and were without collaterals.

c. The exchange wanted to make a very high turnover. Thus, illegal contracts were going on. It was a type of borrowing–lending racket that was run by the Exchange where retail investors and HNIs invested through member brokers.

d. Brokers were getting brokerage of 1-2%. Brokers or investors no one did any due diligence. The scam was as big as Rs. 5,600 crores.

Unfolding Of Fraud

The fraud came to light when the physical deliveries could not be given. The warehouses were empty. Warehouse receipts were not backed by any physical commodity. Thus, when investors went for taking delivery, the warehouses were short of physical goods.

Consequences

a. EOW Mumbai arrested 3 Brokers

b. SEBI issued notices to 300 Brokers

Relevant Sections Of The Indian Penal Code (Ipc) Involved

Section 420 (Cheating), 477A (Falsification of Accounts), 406 (Criminal Breach of Trust), 120B (Criminal Conspiracy), 471 (Using as genuine a forged document or electronic record), 467 (creating false documents), 403 (Dishonest misappropriation of property).

References

www.economictimes.indiatimes.com, www.indianexpress.com, www.ndtv.com

Case Study 49: Diversion Of Bank Funds Through Shell Companies For Personal Gains

Modus Operandi: Borrowing loans and misappropriating the loan funds, Diverting money to shell companies

Profit & Loss Account items involved: Sales to shell companies and other income

Balance Sheet items involved: Debtors (shell companies) and Loans from Banks

Company Involved: ABC Limited (Names changed)

Introduction

ABC Limited is a listed public company. It had an average turnover of around US$ 1500 million p.a. over a period of the last 10 years. The company had taken a loan of US$ 110 million from a bank based on such huge turnover and hypothecated its inventory, debtors, etc.

Fraud

The company reported huge losses for the first time in FY 2015-16. From FY 2009-10 to FY 2015-16, Turnover of the company increased by 100% in 7 years. Operating profit started becoming negative from FY 2011-12. The company could show profits up to FY 2014-15 only because of other incomes. In FY 2015-16, other incomes were a meager figure, it reported a huge loss for the first time in FY 2015-16. Debtors were outstanding for a long time. Loans were increasing every year and so does the interest on the loans, leading to very high expenses.

Unfolding Of Fraud

The non-consortium had appointed a forensic firm to conduct a forensic audit and to find the possible fraud & misappropriation that the company might have committed.

Upon analyzing the long overdue debtors, it was surprising to discover that these top debtors of the companies had common Directors, common Auditors, and common Registered addresses, among other connections.

Furthermore, through the use of digital and social media platforms such as Facebook, LinkedIn, etc., it was found that these directors/employees were either past or present employees of the company. Indirectly, these companies were controlled by the directors of ABC Ltd.

From the debtors' company's financial statements, it was observed that their paid-up share capital was only US$ 0.1 million, and they had booked significant losses in their balance sheets. This implied that the turnover shown by these debtor companies was merely on paper, aiming to create an illusion of substantial turnover to renew and enhance bank loans.

In the study of financial statements of these debtor companies, it was found that a substantial amount of funds had been diverted to related parties and stocks had been written off as non-moving, resulting in substantial losses. As a result, the company attempted to camouflage fraud as non-recovery of debtors or business failure.

Consequences

The analysis established a conspiracy and connivance between management and its associates to deceive the bank and misuse its funds. Accordingly, criminal complaints were filed against the defaulting company.

Note: The proofread version addresses some punctuation and grammar errors to improve clarity and flow. However, if this text is part of a legal or official document, it is essential to consult a legal professional for accuracy and adherence to specific legal language requirements.

Relevant Section Of The Indian Penal Code (IPC) Involved

Section 420 (Cheating), 120B (Criminal Conspiracy), 477A (Falsification of Accounts), 406 (Criminal Breach of Trust), 403 (Dishonest misappropriation of property).

ABC Limited
Balance Sheet (Standalone) (US$ in millions)

Particulars	2009-10	2010-11	2011-12	2012-13	2013-14	2014-15	2015-16
Sources of Funds							
Share Capital	8.43	6.85	6.87	6.88	6.88	6.88	6.88
Reserves & Surplus	184.05	208.72	213.82	229.74	226.96	213.88	113.51
Net worth	192.48	215.58	220.68	236.62	233.85	220.76	120.39
Secured Loans	68.53	65.64	79.97	103.74	104.79	69.96	42.19
Unsecured Loans	166.10	252.04	378.74	440.13	152.02	254.83	409.19
Total Loans	234.63	317.67	458.71	543.87	256.81	324.80	451.38
Non Current Liabilities & Provisions	16.87	21.73	28.78	27.46	28.49	46.20	29.19
Total	443.98	554.98	708.17	807.95	519.14	591.75	600.96
Application of Funds							
Net Fixed Assets	202.49	228.52	258.20	269.31	263.95	248.07	235.11
Investment	18.13	18.68	21.03	26.11	32.33	28.18	22.87
Other Non Current Assets	-	11.34	8.47	11.89	9.70	13.52	17.97
Current Assets	529.37	696.52	980.57	1,135.39	925.04	1,097.12	1,071.57
Current Liabilities (Other than Bank Loan)	291.57	371.71	529.25	606.89	675.43	756.12	707.63
Current liabilities - Bank Loan	14.46	28.41	31.01	27.88	36.47	39.05	39.00
Total Current Liabilities	306.03	400.12	560.26	634.77	711.90	795.17	746.63
Net Current Assets	223.34	296.41	420.31	500.61	213.14	301.95	324.94
Misc. Expenditure Without Written off	0.02	0.03	0.17	0.03	0.02	0.03	0.07
Total	443.98	554.98	708.17	807.95	519.14	591.75	600.96

ABC Limited
Statement of Profit and Loss (Standalone) (US$ in millions)

Particulars	2009-10	2010-11	2011-12	2012-13	2013-14	2014-15	2015-16
Sales	1,341.11	1,650.35	2,583.81	2,591.76	2,405.96	2,775.65	2,773.46
Total Expenditure	1,315.41	1,620.99	2,533.33	2,572.48	2,386.73	2,778.56	2,799.78
EBIDTA	25.70	29.36	50.48	19.28	19.23	-2.91	-26.31
Depreciation	12.03	11.99	14.07	15.43	16.45	14.80	14.99
EBIT	13.67	17.37	36.41	3.85	2.78	-17.71	-41.30
Interest Cost	6.74	11.79	52.13	31.61	53.05	46.23	61.87
Operating Profit	6.93	5.58	-15.72	-27.76	-50.27	-63.94	-103.18
Operating Cash Flow	18.65	-88.23	90.62	-145.08	345.12	-50.79	NA
Other Income	19.97	27.22	38.27	58.11	54.15	65.40	7.08
Extraordinary Item	0.35	-	-	-	1.11	6.49	2.39
PBT	27.25	32.80	22.55	30.35	4.98	7.95	-93.70
Tax	10.00	11.48	10.60	6.73	3.63	1.97	-7.99
PAT	17.25	21.32	11.95	23.62	1.35	5.99	-85.72
PAT Margin (%)	0.01	0.01	0	0.01	0	0	-0.03
Sales Growth (%)	0.0%	23.1%	56.6%	0.3%	-7.2%	15.4%	-0.1%
EBITDA Growth (%)	0.0%	14.3%	71.9%	-61.8%	-0.3%	-115.1%	805.5%
PAT Growth (%)	0.0%	23.6%	-43.9%	97.6%	-94.3%	343.1%	-1532.0%

Sr.	Name of Companies	Address	Name of Auditor	Directors of the company	As on 29/02/2016 Audited by CA	As on 31/03/2016 as per list provided	Advances Given as on 31/03/2016	Remark (Findings from Social media)
1	DK Impex Pvt Ltd	7/B, Rose Villa, Mumbai	M/s AK Wala & Co.	1)Mr. NA Pakwal (10/03/2010); 2)Mr. AB Agarwal (01/09/2014); 3)Mr. SS Gangrade; 4)Mr.VK Gupta	10.69	19.75	2.30	Mr. AB Agrawal Employee of ABC Ltd
2	STU Multitrade Pvt Ltd	Office No. 46, Flower Apt, Mumbai	M/s. GH Hupta & Co.	1)Mr. RP Hardira (01/10/2012); 2)Mr. AB Agrawal (10/10/2014)	2.43	23.58	-	
3	PQR Marketing Pvt Ltd	Office No. 36, Flower Apt, Mumbai	M/s AK Wala & Co.	1)Mr. PP Napar (01/12/2010); 2)Mr. SL Jain (01/10/2012)	13.64	24.98	1.40	
4	FGH Impex Pvt Ltd	10GH, Jasmine Apt, Mumbai	M/s. GH Hupta & Co.	1)Mr. PP Napar (01/09/2014); 2)Mr. DK Gupta (31/03/2000)	21.04	24.12	-	Mr. PP Napar Employee of ABC Ltd
5	SQR Trading Pvt Ltd	7/B, Rose Villa, Mumbai	M/s. CJ Jain & Co.	1)Mr. SH Kurkute (05/01/2011); 2)Mr. PP Napar (15/07/2015); 3)Mr. VY Sharma (20/01/2003)	-	-	6.00	
6	RST Impex Pvt Ltd	10GH, Jasmine Apt, Mumbai	M/s. GH Hupta & Co.	1)Mr. RH Gupta (25/10/2002); 2)Mr. RS Patwal (18/09/2002)	0.98	16.59	-	Mr. RH Gupta Employee of ABC Ltd
7	RRR Trading Pvt Ltd	Office No. 36, Flower Apt, Mumbai	M/s AK Wala & Co.	1)Mr. NA Pakwal (10/03/2010); 2)Mr. RH Gupta (24/03/2003)	-	-	1.55	
8	GHI Multitrade Pvt Ltd	Office No. 46, Flower Apt, Mumbai	M/s. GH Hupta & Co.	1)Mr. SD Parashar (01/10/2009); 2)Mr. PH Gupta (17/06/2006)	3.70	24.75	-	
9	ACD Trading Pvt Ltd	Office No. 36, Flower Apt, Mumbai	M/s. SBP Satidar & Co.	1)Mr. SD Parashar (30/03/2009); 2)Mr. RH Gupta (01/01/2004)	-	-	6.57	Mr. SD Parashar Employee of ABC Ltd
10	MNO Multitrade Pvt Ltd	Office No. 36, Flower Apt, Mumbai	M/s. GH Hupta & Co.	1)Mr. SD Parashar (01/10/2009); 2)Mr. PH Gupta (17/06/2002)	-	26.40	-	
11	XYZ Marktrade Pvt Ltd	7/B, Rose Villa, Mumbai	M/s. SBP Satidar & Co.	1)Mr. SL Jain (01/09/2014); 2)Mr. RR Khande (15/03/2009); 3)Mr. SS Gangrade	15.38	-	-	Mr. SS Gangrade Employee of ABC Ltd
	TOTAL				68.26	160.16	17.82	

Total Diff: 91.90   Total: 177.9

Case Study 50: Tyco Scandal – Hitting Two Birds With A Single Stone

Modus Operandi: Floating different schemes in the name of employees with the intent to diversify the funds for KMP

Profit & Loss Account: Loans to employees written off

Balance Sheet: Loans to employees and KMPs, Purchase of assets, Share Capital (Employees Stock options)

Company Involved: Tyco International

Introduction

Tyco International was incorporated in 1960 in Massachusetts. In 1982 it had divisions like fire protection, electronics, and packaging. In the 1990s the company again reorganized and included products like electrical and electronic components, health care, and specialty products.

In 1992, Leo Dennis Kozlowski became the CEO after climbing up the corporate ladder from executive, president, and CFO. He had a very aggressive approach toward mergers and acquisitions during his CEO tenure. Thus, the business was diversified due to many acquisitions.

Fraud

He appointed directors from his own group of people. Following frauds were committed anyt Tyco International:

a) When Tyco was growing and its office was moved from New York to Florida and thus, many employees had to be relocated. To make it comfortable for employees, a scheme was floated for employees, where they can take loans at very low rates of interest/no interest from the company. The Management took undue advantage of the scheme. Later relocation loans forgiveness program was floated by them and thus, the money was siphoned by them (this relocation loans forgiveness scheme was kept a secret)

b) Tyco Key Employees corporate loan program was floated so that key employees could purchase stock options and can pay the tax on the same. But they misappropriated and siphoned the funds from the company for buying luxurious personal assets like mansions, yachts, and fine arts. Other employees who came to know about this, did not speak as they were financially benefited as compensation for not speaking.

c) They sold their own properties to Tyco at 3 times their actual prices, thus gaining out of that.

d) They also discharged some employees without notice when he found that some of the merged companies did not perform well and could not produce revenue. Employees who gave unfavorable reviews to Tyco were also fired.

e) A lot of subsidiary companies were opened some of which were only opened which benefitted some key managerial personnel which were hidden even from the auditors (by limiting the scope of internal audits).

f) They artificially inflated the value stock of the company and sold their stock which was not allowed to be sold and earned $ 430 million.

g) The CEO also evaded a sales tax of $ 1 million on the purchase of artworks.

Unfolding Of Fraud

In early 2002, when Tyco acquired several companies and started suffering losses, restructuring and demergers took place. Securities & Exchange Commission initiated an inquiry into Tyco's affairs. Thus, fraud started unfolding.

Consequences

The masterminds were sentenced to 25 years in jail for $ 600 million fraud.

Relevant Section Of Indian Penal Code (IPC) Involved

Section 420 (Cheating), 406 (Criminal Breach of Trust), 477A (Falsification of Accounts), 120B (Criminal Conspiracy), 466 (An aggregated form of forgery), 403 (Dishonest misappropriation of property), 471 (The creation of documents for the purpose of cheating).

References

www.nytimes.com

www.nbcnews.com

www.lawteacher,net

Chapter 9

Forensic Accounting and Investigation Standards prescribed by ICAI

The Institute of Chartered Accountants of India (ICAI), through its Digital Accounting and Assurance Board (DAAB), has prescribed twenty Forensic Accounting and Investigation Standards, which will be effective from 1st July 2023.

The main objective of introducing these standards is to provide adequate scope for professional judgment while simultaneously applying the principles laid down in the standards to handle unique situations and specific circumstances. The forensic accounting and investigation standards serve as a predefined framework to ensure a consistent application of best principles, best practices, and high-level quality when conducting forensic investigations across different types of forensic accounting and investigation engagements.

It is the duty of professionals to comply with these standards and apply the basic principles of forensic accounting and investigation. By doing so, they can provide comfort and assurance to the appointor regarding the reasonable quality of the forensic auditor during the course of forensic accounting and investigations.

The twenty headers of the Forensic Accounting and Investigation standards are as follows:

FAIS No.	Forensic Accounting And Investigation Standard
FAIS 110	Nature of Engagement
FAIS 120	Fraud Risk
FAIS 130	Laws and Regulations
FAIS 140	Applying Hypotheses
FAIS 210	Engagement Objectives
FAIS 220	Engagement Acceptance and Appointment
FAIS 230	Using the work of an Expert
FAIS 240	Engaging with Agencies
FAIS 250	Communication with Stakeholders
FAIS 310	Planning the Assignment
FAIS 320	Evidence and Documentation
FAIS 330	Conducting Work Procedures
FAIS 340	Conducting Interviews
FAIS 350	Review and Supervision
FAIS 360	Testifying Before a Competent Authority
FAIS 410	Applying Data Analysis
FAIS 420	Evidence Gathering in Digital Domain

FAIS 430	Loans and Borrowings
FAIS 510	Reporting Results
FAIS 610	Quality Control

The application of the above twenty standards which is required to be followed by the forensic accounting and investigation auditors will give boost to the Indian Economy not only in finding financial frauds but also helping the economy in a robust manner to prevent the frauds.

Bibliography/Webliography

www.business-standard.com

www.ndtv.com

www.livemint.com

www.economictimes.indiatimes.com

www.lawstreetindia.com

www.news18.com

www.ipleaders.in

www.indianexpress.com

www.businessinsider.in

www.businesstoday.in

www.financialexpress.com

www.hindustantimes.com

www.thehindu.com

www.thetimesofindia.indiatimes.com

www.indigolearn.com

www.moneylife.in

www.indiakanoon.org

www.lawteacher.net

www.en.wikipedia.org

www.whitecollarfraud.com

www.nytimes.com

www.nbcnews.com

www.lawteacher,net

www.investopedia.com

Glossary

Amortisation the systematic writing off of the cost, less any residual value, of an intangible asset over its estimated useful life.

Associate Company a company in which another company can exercise significant influence. Such influence generally arises from a greater than 20% voting power in the associated company.

Audit Committee a subcommittee of an organisation's board of directors that is charged with supervising the financial reporting system.

Audit Trail is a documented flow of a transaction. It is used to investigate how a source document was converted into an accounting entry.

Cash Flow Statement a statement that summarizes the company's cash and bank inflows and outflows during the financial year. It helps in providing insights into company's liquidity and financial health.

Cash Larceny the theft of an organisation's cash after it has been recorded in the books of accounts.

Circular Transactions (Round Tripping) an artificial transaction between companies generally falling under the same ownership/ group. Funds are transferred from one company to another but no exchange of goods or service takes place.

Collateralized borrowings a loan that is secured by a specific asset; if the borrower defaults, the lender takes possession of that asset as repayment.

Concealed liabilities and expenses a type of financial statement fraud scheme in which the perpetrators intentionally under mentions or omits liabilities and/ or expenses from the organization's financial statements.

Connivance is an act of agreement between two or more people involved in an illegal activity for personal gains.

Contingent Liabilities are future liabilities which may occur or not depending on occurrence or non-occurrence of certain events.

Corruption fraud schemes in which an employee uses his position in a business transaction in a way that breaches his duty to his employer for the purpose of obtaining a personal benefit or someone else, examples include bribery, extortion and conflicts of interest.

Criminal conspiracy an agreement between two or more people to commit an illegal act to attain common object.

Debt rating a measurement of the credit worthiness of a corporation's or government's debt securities.

Debt servicing cost the cash flow required to meet the organisation's interest expenses and principal payments during a specific time period.

Depreciation the systematic writing off of the cost, less any residual value of a fixed asset over its estimated useful life.

Double pledged assets same asset mortgaged to more than one lender or banker.

Embezzlement the wrongful grabbing or conversion of the property of another person for the wrongdoer's advantage.

Fictitious Parties are parties that do not exist in reality and are created to misappropriate funds. Transaction with such parties only occur on paper but in reality, no services/goods are exchanged.

Fictitious revenue the recording of sales of goods or services that never happened.

Fiduciary duty some duties imposed by law that people in a position of trust such as officers, directors, key management personnel of a corporation or business and agent or brokers owe to their principals or employers; the principal fiduciary duties are loyalty, integrity and honesty.

Financial statement analysis a detailed examination of the comparison of each item on the financial statements using techniques such as ratio analysis and sampling.

Financial statement fraud the deliberate misrepresentation of the financial condition of an enterprise through the intentional misstatement or omission and commission of amounts or disclosures in the financial statements to cheat financial statement users.

Forensic Audit is a technique used to analyze, investigate and report financial data or information of a company in manner acceptable in the court of law.

Fraudulent disbursement a scheme in which an employee illegally or improperly causes the distribution of funds in a way that appears to be legitimate but it is not so.

Fraudulent write-off a method used to conceal the theft of assets by justifying their non recovery on the books (e.g., as lost, destroyed, slow moving or scrap in case of inventory, or as bad debts or sales returns/ allowances in the case of accounts receivable)

Fund Flow Statement is a statement that analyzes changes in the financial position between two balance sheet dates. It consists of two sides: a.) Sources – Money coming into business b.) Application – Money going out of business.

Ghost employee an individual on the payroll of a company who does not actually work for the company but their name reflects in payroll.

Impaired asset an asset whose fair market value is determined to be lesser than actual and expected to remain less than the value recorded on the books.

Improper asset valuation the fraudulent statement of the book value of an asset (usually inventory accounts receivable or fixed assets.)

Improper disclosure the fraudulent omission or commission or intentionally misleading wording of any of the disclosures, supporting schedules or other such information required to be included in the financial statements.

Induce (Inducement) is an act of persuading a person to carry out an act which is not beneficial to such person.

Intangible asset an asset that is not in a position to be seen or touched such as patent, trademark goodwill or copyright.

Internal controls policies and procedures design and implemented to ensure the organization's operational efficiency, transparency and effectiveness on reliability of financial reporting and statutory compliance thereof.

Lapping the crediting of one account through the abstraction of money from another account typically to hide or conceal incoming payments.

Letter of Credit a letter from a bank guaranteeing that a buyer's payment to a seller will be received on time and for the correct amount.

Liability/ expense omission a deliberate and purposeful attempt to conceal from the financial statements of all liability or expense that has already been incurred.

Long term debt liabilities that are not due and payable for more than a year.

Management representation letter a letter issued by management to the auditor clarifying the authenticity, sufficiency completeness and appropriateness of the organization's financial statements.

Money laundering a process in which illegally obtained money is introduced by criminals into legal channels.

Networth is the financial strength of an entity i.e., surplus assets owned after deducting all liabilities.

Overstatement type of financial statement fraud in which one or more items on the financial statements are reported as greater than the actual amounts. Figures are overstated to attract the investors. Revenue and assets accounts are the most common subjects of overstatements.

Qualified audit report a report in which auditor qualifies if certain items of the financial statements which are not stated as per accounting standards. The auditors qualify any item in the report when he concludes that the figures mentioned in the financial statements are not correct or not supported with proper documentation.

Red Flag is a sign or an indicator that a particular item is not consistent with the other balances or items of the financial statement. It is a pre-signal of fraudulent activities.

Related party transaction a transaction that occurs when a company does business with another entity whose management or operating policies can be controlled or significantly influenced by the company or its common directors or by some other party in common.

Shell Companies are companies holding significant investments in other companies to influence or hide true owners of the company.

Short term debt liabilities that are due and payable within a year.

Skimming theft of cash prior to its entry into the books of accounts.

Tangible Asset an asset that is able to be seen, touched and/or physically measured such as cash inventory land & building and equipment.

Tax Avoidance the use of legal means to reduce a taxpayer's tax liability.

Tax evasion the intentional and purposely use of illegal means to reduce a taxpayer's tax liability.

Timing differences a method of financial statement manipulation in which revenue or expenses are intentionally recorded in an improper period to reflect rosy picture of the organization.

Understatement type of financial statement fraud in which one or more items on the financial statements are reported as less than the actual amounts. Figures are understated to minimize tax liability. Expense and liability accounts are the most common subjects of understatements.

Unqualified audit report an auditor's report stating that the financial statements are presented fairly in all material respects and same is true and correct.

Wire fraud the use of electronic communications to perpetrate a scheme to defraud a victim of money or property by using illegal means.

Wrongful Gain is a gain by a person through unlawful means to which the person gaining is not legally entitled.

INDEX

A

Accumulated Deficit 137

Acquisitions 204, 208, 281

Administrative Expenditure 15, 20, 95, 161, 248

Artificial booking of income 89

Artificial Growth In Sales 271

Artificially Inflated The Value Of Stock 282

Associate Company 8, 60, 73, 76, 91, 94, 98, 99, 102, 109, 117, 214, 215, 216, 217

Audit Trail 64, 223

Auditors report under CARO 31

B

Bad Debts 16, 21, 67, 77, 99, 100, 143, 144, 241, 242

Bank Balances 9, 78, 161

Bank Overdraft 13, 85, 114, 126

Banking Fraud Investigation 121

Bankruptcy Proceedings 167, 177

Bogus 67, 69, 78, 85, 93, 99, 233, 236, 254

C

Cash flow statement 2, 24

Cash Sales 89, 270, 271

Cheating 56, 202, 207, 214, 216, 219, 220

Circular Transactions (Round Tripping) 183, 184, 189, 206

Collateral 116, 117, 166, 190, 260, 261, 273

Commission 21, 46, 89, 95, 97, 128, 158, 212, 241, 242, 256, 264, 273, 283

Common Auditors 276

Common Directors 60, 78, 79, 80, 81, 83, 84, 87, 88, 89, 90, 91, 93, 96, 97, 99, 146, 170, 276

Common Registered Addresses 88, 276

Company's Funds (Misappropriation/ siphoning/ diversion) 152, 154, 155, 161, 175, 260

Concealment 52, 54, 66, 114, 117, 138, 174, 177

Connivance 52, 211, 212, 277

Consolidated Financials Statements (CFS) 109, 173, 208

Contingent Liabilities 2, 4, 28, 85, 144, 165

Copyright 5, 7, 72

Creation Of Documents 136, 139, 142, 145, 274, 283

Criminal Breach Of Trust 55, 56

Criminal Conspiracy 53, 54, 163, 186, 200, 207, 215, 218, 239

Criminal Liability of Auditors 39

Criminal Liability of directors 42

Criminal Prosecuton 131, 132, 133

Current Assets 3, 4, 8, 9, 18, 33, 39, 74, 113, 114, 118

Current Liability 3, 4, 12, 13, 39, 84, 113, 114

D

Default in repayment of loan 34

Defer Revenue 150, 208, 209

Deferred Expenses 137, 138

Depreciation 16, 21, 66

Disclosure of transactions 35

Dishonest Dealing in Property 54, 148, 151, 154, 157, 160

Disposal Of Stocks 200

Dividend 10, 11, 16,17, 23, 24, 26, 58, 152, 153, 231

E

Early Warning Signals 116

Embezzlement 192, 228, 229, 246

Equity Shares 10, 12, 73, 146

Evasion Of Tax 69, 70

Evergreening 184, 204, 249

F

Fake Bills 84, 88, 96

Fake Purchase 91, 228, 238

Fake Sales 161, 238, 260, 261

Fictitious Bank Account 260, 262

Fictitious Companies 138, 151

Fictitious Parties 151, 179

Financial Irregularities 171, 176

Foreign Associates 80, 158

Foreign Companies 62, 63, 90, 99, 107, 108, 225

Foreign Subsidiaries 36, 69, 74, 80, 99, 101, 102, 137, 216, 260

Forensic Audit 36, 51, 169, 183, 200, 239, 252, 276

Forensic Auditor 176, 206, 217, 243, 251, 252, 286

Forgery 57, 58, 163, 164, 181, 186, 187, 200, 213, 229, 232, 237, 246, 249, 255, 263, 272, 283

Fraud Reporting 35

Fraudulently 7, 49, 52, 53, 54, 57, 58, 62, 63, 67, 69, 79, 116, 128, 138, 167, 185, 186, 204, 205, 212, 252

Fund flow statement 24, 25, 26

G

Ghost Employees 95, 96, 155, 156, 161, 162

Goodwill 5, 6, 8, 71

Gross Profit 15, 19, 74, 111, 112

I

Inappropriate Accounting Techniques 267, 268

Independent Directors 48, 49

Induce 56, 167

Inflated Sales 260, 155, 254

Initial Public Offering (IPO) 35, 140, 141, 142, 270, 271

Insolvency and Bankrupty code (IBC) 129, 130

Intellectual Properties 5, 8

Intercorporate Deposits 98, 146

Internal Control 63, 64, 89, 149

Inventory 9, 13, 32, 74, 75, 76, 113, 114, 116, 118, 138, 169, 170, 208, 209, 239, 252, 272, 273, 275

Investment Written Off 22, 68, 69, 78, 79, 102

J

Journal Entries 14, 66, 67, 76, 144, 208

L

Lifting of Corporate Veil 43

Loans To Employees 9, 281

Loans To Shell Companies 202, 238, 264

Long term borrowing 3, 12, 83, 204

M

Manipulation Of Accounts 74, 140, 143, 208, 223, 239, 254, 262, 267

MCA website 103

Money Laundering 59, 63, 81, 83, 149, 167, 177, 190, 192, 193, 226, 235, 236, 239

N

Net Profit 16, 23, 24, 84, 112

Networth 1, 3, 4, 10, 11, 22, 38, 39, 109, 127

Non Performing Assets (NPA) 126, 129, 183, 195, 196, 238, 243, 249

Non-Recovery Of Debtors 170, 276

Notes of accounts 2, 4, 28, 165

P

Paper Turnover 238

Patent 5, 7, 71

Personal Assets 66, 146, 154, 161, 260, 261, 282

Possessing Of Stolen Property 56, 148, 151, 154, 157, 160, 224

Preference Share Capital 10, 81, 146

Premature Expenses 208, 209

Prospectus 43, 147

Provision For Doubtful Debts 67, 68, 143, 169

Q

Qualified Audit Report 38

R

Ratio Analysis 111

Rebates From Creditors (Kickback) 69, 244, 262, 270

Reconciliation 78, 136

Red Flag 68, 80, 96, 111, 112, 113, 114, 115, 251

Reserves 1, 3, 4, 11, 23, 26, 79, 82, 115, 143, 144, 155, 169, 267

Restructuring 182, 283, 175

Role of Directors 41

S

Schemes 73, 74, 136, 256, 281

Shareholders Fund 4, 146

Shell Companies 59, 66, 76, 88, 135, 136, 137, 149, 179, 180, 184, 186, 192, 202, 235, 236, 238, 245, 264, 265, 275

Significant Losses 22, 276

Slow Boating 141

Subsidiary Companies 22, 60, 61, 62, 76, 86, 102, 261, 282

Sundry Balances written bank 16, 20, 68, 93

T

Trade Payables 13, 84

Trade Receivables 9, 13, 76

Trademark 5, 7, 71, 72

U

Unrealistic Profit Targets 142, 268

Use Of Proceeds Of Crime 177, 185, 186, 203, 236

Using A Genuine As Forged Document/ Electronic Record 58, 181, 187, 213, 230, 249, 255, 272, 274

V

Very High Returns 158, 256, 258

W

Wilful Defaulters 34, 128

Window Dressing 135, 137, 169, 205, 261, 267

Write-Offs Of Stock 208, 209

Write-Offs Of Debtors 77, 170

Write-Offs Of Investment 68, 78, 79

Wrongful Gain 52, 53, 186

Wrongful Loss 52, 53, 63, 100, 101, 102, 186

www.ingramcontent.com/pod-product-compliance
Lightning Source LLC
LaVergne TN
LVHW091708070526
838199LV00050B/2311